Copyright 2021 by Dr. Archibald Johansson - All rights reserved.

This document is geared towards providing exact and reliable information in regard to the topic and issue covered. The publication is sold on the idea that the publisher is not required to render an accounting, officially permitted, or otherwise, qualified services. If advice is necessary, legal or professional, a practiced individual in the profession should be ordered.

From a Declaration of Principles which was accepted and approved equally by a Committee of the American Bar Association and a Committee of Publishers and Associations.

In no way is it legal to reproduce, duplicate, or transmit any part of this document by either electronic means or in printed format. Recording of this publication is strictly prohibited and any storage of this document is not allowed unless with written permission from the publisher. All rights reserved.

The information provided herein is stated to be truthful and consistent, in that any liability, in terms of inattention or otherwise, by any usage or abuse of any policies, processes, or Instructions: contained within is the solitary and utter responsibility of the recipient reader. Under no circumstances will any legal responsibility or blame be held against the publisher for any reparation, damages, or monetary loss due to the information herein, either directly or indirectly.

By continuing with this book, readers agree that the author is under no circumstances responsible for any losses, indirect or direct, that are incurred as a result of the information presented in this document, including, but not limited to inaccuracies, omissions and errors. Respective authors own all copyrights not held by the publisher. The information herein is offered for informational purposes solely and is universal as so.

The presentation of the information is without a contract or any type of guarantee assurance.

The information herein is offered for informational purposes solely and is universal as so. The presentation of the information is without contract or any type of guarantee assurance. Readers acknowledge that the author is not engaging in the rendering of legal, financial, medical or professional advice. Please consult a licensed professional before attempting any techniques outlined in this book.

CONTENTS

INTRODUCTION 9
CAUSES AND SYMPTOMS 10
    Risk factors 12
    Happy liver happy life 12
WHAT TO EAT AND WHAT NOT? 15
    Protein 15
    Carbohydrates 17
    Fat 18
    Fruit and vegetable 20
    Fiber 21
    Sweets, Coffee and Alcohol 22
Tips and tricks and how to use this book 24
APPETIZER RECIPES 28
        Banana Walnut Pancakes 29
        Barley Oats Granola with Almond 31
        Quinoa Coconut Chocolate Muffins 33
        Crab, Dill Fritters 35
        Buckwheat Strawberry Pancakes 37
        Tangy Lime-Garlic Kale Shrimps 39
        Apple Muffins with Cinnamon 41
        Millet Barley Pancakes 43

Roasted Potatoes with Garlic and Parsley and Rosemary 45

Mixed Flour Banana Bread 47

Grilled Tangy and Sweet Pineapple 49

Breakfast Farro Porridge 52

Stuffed Mushrooms with Herbs 54

Chicken Tenders with Pineapple 56

Fresh Fruit Kebabs 58

Maple Syrup-Glazed Herbed Sweet Potatoes 60

Zucchini Chips with Parmesan Cheese 62

Grilled Spicy Sweet Potato with Garlic 64

Potato Cauliflower Pancakes 66

Carrot Parsnips Tzimmes with Parsley 68

Chia Seed Parfaits with Lime and Berries 70

Banana Quinoa 72

Omelet with Brussels Sprouts & Asiago Cheese 74

Vegetable Scrambled Eggs 76

Sweet Potato Garlicky Omelet 78

Herb Frittatas with Zucchini and Tomato 80

MAIN MEALS 82

Ginger Tempeh and Vegetable Stir-Fry 83

Grilled Turkey Teriyaki 85

Sautéed Turkey and Cabbage 87

Ginger Glazed Tuna 89

Egg Fried Quinoa 91

Garlic Turkey Breasts with Lemon 93

Maple Syrup-Orange Glazed Salmon 95

Garlicky Barley and Pinto Beans 97

Creamy Broccoli and Sweet Potato Soup 99

Meatballs with Ginger 101

Mahi-Mahi Salad-Stuffed Avocado 103

Cod Salad with Eggs 105

Chicken Chili 107

Kale and Cottage Pasta 109

Couscous Salad 111

Chicken Fajita Bowl 113

Quinoa Vegetable Soup with Beans 115

Red Lentil and Chickpeas Soup 117

Carrot and Zucchini Soup 119

Hemp Broiled Tilapia with Ginger 121

Baked Chicken with Barley 123

Fresh Kale Garlic Soup 125

Glazed Tempeh 127

Vegetable Stew 129

Turkey and Orzo Soup 131

DESSERT RECIPES 133

Nutmeg Apple Frozen Yogurt 134

Chocolate Cookies without Flour 136

Chocolate Biscotti with Walnuts 138

Chilled Banana Pudding 140

Oatmeal Cookies with Nutmeg- Apricots 142

Almond Butter- Quinoa Energy Balls 144

Almond Barley Pudding 146

Pecans-Cinnamon Pumpkin Custards 148

Coconut Mug Brownie 151

No-Bake Cookies 153

Mini Fruit Pizzas With Pears 155

Blueberry Oats Bars 157

Green Tea Maple syrup Frozen Yogurt 159

Raspberry Cobbler 161

Blueberry Ice Cream 163

Baked Pears with Quinoa 165

Quinoa Cookies 168

Delicious Nutmeg Baked Peaches 170

Zucchini Cookies 172

Yummy Red Dragon Fruit Sorbet 174

Papaya and Mint Sorbet 176

Butternut Squash Pie 178

Banana Oat Bars 180

Orange Sesame Seed Biscotti 182

Gingerbread Balls 184
SMOOTHIES AND DRINKS 186
    Mango Ginger Smoothie 187
    Kiwi Strawberry Banana Smoothie... 189
    Berry Mint Smoothie 191
    Banana Protein Smoothie 193
    Kale and Chia Seed Green Smoothie 195
    Banana Cauliflower Smoothie 197
    Pineapple Smoothie.. 199
    Strawberry Raspberry Smoothie 201
    Green Tea Peach Smoothie 203
    Mermaid Smoothie Bowl.. 205
    Spinach Protein Smoothie 207
    Pumpkin and Pear Smoothie 209
    Cucumber Breeze Smoothie... 211
    Blueberry Banana Smoothies 213
    Pomegranate Blackberry Smoothie... 215
    Green Monster 217
    Cranberry Ginger Smoothie... 219
    Almond Apple Smoothie 221
    Citrus Tangy Boosting Smoothie 223
    Vanilla Peach Avocado Smoothie 225
    Immunity Boosting Smoothie 227

 Apple Cucumber Refresher 229

 Blueberry- Carrots Smoothie 231

 Beet and Strawberry Smoothie 233

 Watermelon Smoothie 235

RECOVERY RECIPES 237

 Homemade Chicken Broth 238

 Homemade Vegetable Stock 240

 Celery Juice 242

 Carrot Juice 243

 Fruit and Vegetable Drink 244

 Warm Apple Juice 245

 Blended Beet and Potato Soup 246

 Potato Spinach Soup 248

 Carrot Soup 250

 Potato and Turnip 252

4-WEEKS MEAL PLAN 253

 1st Week Meal Plan 254

 2nd Week Meal Plan 255

 3rd Week Meal Plan 256

 4th Week Meal Plan 257

INTRODUCTION

The gallbladder is a 5 to 10 centimeter-sized sac-like organ in the right upper abdomen that stores bile formed in the liver. Bile plays an important role in our digestive system. It is made up of cholesterol, bile salts and waste products. If the bile is imbalanced, crystals form, which stick together and thus form stones; however, it can also be in the form of sludge or sand.

Gallstones are a reasonably common disease as they are found in 20% of women over the age of 40 and in 10% of men of the same age. They are related to family burden, childbirth, diet and body constitution. Gallstones can be completely asymptomatic, but they can also cause several problems. Most people with gallstones have no troubles at all. According to research, only about 20 % of people with gallstones will have troubles in the next 15 years.

If severe symptoms occur, such as abdominal pain, digestion issues, inflammation, vomiting and others, the operation in order to remove a gallbladder might be a necessity. Gallbladder removal procedure, also known as cholecystectomy, is one of the most common operations in the USA, as well as around the world.

You can live normally without your gallbladder. Your body just needs time to adapt to functioning and digesting food without it. Dietary adjustments are, therefore, a necessary step to recovery.

This book offers you more than 111 delicious and easy recipes to ease you on the path to complete recovery after the operation. But it can also be used as a preventive measure for all who wish to avoid gallbladder troubles completely and live healthily and happily instead!

CAUSES AND SYMPTOMS

Gallbladder problems are caused by unhealthy liver and digestive system. If the liver is not healthy, it will form poor quality bile. As already said, crystals can form from poor quality and imbalanced bile. The crystals then stick together and form gallstones.

Usually, problems with gallstones are related to the movement of the stones when the bile is excreted. When the gallbladder contracts, in order to release bile, the stones can close the bile duct. This can be felt like an attack of bile cramps, with pain under the right ribs that can radiate to the right shoulder or back. The pain is usually constant, can last for an hour or more and then gradually resolve. Nausea and vomiting can occur. If the pain does not subside and fever and vomiting occur, we might be in serious trouble and medical assistance shall be sought.

Such serious symptoms are usually the consequence of gallstones, which are not eliminated from the gallbladder spontaneously. The stones can prevent the outflow of bile from the liver, which results in jaundice. Stones can also clog the pancreas, which can cause inflammation. Inflammation (pancreatitis) is a disease with a very unpredictable course. It can require long-term hospital treatment with many complications, and in its worst form has a fairly high mortality rate.

In case of severe troubles, the gallbladder is removed. The liver, however, continues to form bile and the bile proceeds to flow into the intestines. But there is a lack of storage for it, as it would in normal circumstances be stored in the gallbladder. Moreover, bile also thickens in the gallbladder, so the lack of the organ might result in a more dilute, watery bile.

Too little or too dilute bile causes a lot of problems. People without gallbladder usually have trouble digesting fatty food due to the lack of bile. This leads to poor digestion, diarrhea, bloating and nausea.

For one, affected people won't be able to digest essential fatty acids, including omega 3 and omega 6 fatty acids. This means that it will be difficult to get enough fat-soluble vitamins such as D, E, A and K. Many antioxidants in vegetables are fat-soluble: lycopene, lutein, carotenoids. If the body does not produce enough bile, it cannot absorb enough of these vital substances. Taking nutritional supplements will not help because even in such a form, without a sufficient amount of bile, the body is unable to absorb them. Some of the most common signs of poor fat metabolism are dry and brittle hair, dry skin and premature skin aging. The nails are thin and also brittle, joint pain occurs. Essential fatty acids are important for good brain function and health, so low mood, excessive anxiety, depression and poor perception can also occur in case of poor metabolism.

Even after removal of the gallbladder, many typical problems recur. Fine sand and stones are now made and located in the liver since there is no other storage left for it, which can impair their functions and is dangerous.

One can live normally without the gallbladder. Bile will flow into the intestines through the bile duct straight from the liver. It takes some time for your stomach to get used to the new digestive conditions. During this time, it is advisable to follow a healthy recovery diet.

Risk factors

Female gender is an important risk factor: women between the ages of 30 and 40 have gallstones three times more often than men, whereas after age 60 women have them only 20 percent more often than men.

Stones often form during pregnancy and during a rapid weight loss - especially dangerous are weight-loss diets with very low-calorie intake. The incidence of gallstones increases with age and is also associated with certain diseases (diabetes, liver cirrhosis, certain medications).

Obesity is another important risk factor, as thick stones are three times more common, and heredity is also important.

But most of all, an unhealthy lifestyle increases the chances of gallstones. An unhealthy lifestyle includes eating a lot of fatty, processed and sugary foods, drinking large amounts of alcohol, dealing with a lot of stress in our lives and lacking exercise.

Happy liver happy life

When problems with the gallbladder occur, they need to be addressed along with liver problems. The gallbladder is just a bag or a reservoir into which liver secretions are poured. Removing the gallbladder because there are gallstones in it is not the long-term solution. Bile, which later forms gallstones, is produced by the liver, so removing the gallstones or gallbladder does not eliminate the ground that caused the gallstones to appear.

The liver is our main cleansing organ, a filter of our body. It provides us with more than 200 functions and is one of the most important organs in our bodies. The liver knows when we're sick and take strong medications, when we're angry when we ate spoiled or unappropriated food when we drank too much alcohol during the holidays, or if we haven't slept in a long time, and so on.

An unhealthy lifestyle burdens our liver and leads to poor liver function. Burdening our liver is thus not good, as optimal liver function is a condition for vitality and health in general. Poor liver function may cause lack of energy, inflammation of the joints, poor digestion, the appearance of allergies, including hay fever, high blood pressure, poor hormonal balance maintenance, diabetes, obesity and even infertility, in addition to gallbladder problems.

To make it clear, gallstones are made by our fault. We created a perfect environment for them to form, by eating inappropriate food, by poor stress management, by exercising too little or not drinking enough liquid.

Thus, strengthening the liver is an integral part of our strategy to eliminate or prevent many problems, including those with the gallbladder. We have to put in the maximum effort to sustain a happy and healthy liver so that our liver will not be fatty; that it will form perfect bile; that the bile will flow freely through our digestive system; that toxic substances will be excreted regularly; that any sand or stones in the liver will dissolve and be excreted regularly; that liver cells will be able to regenerate and perform many functions.

WHAT TO EAT AND WHAT NOT?

The food that we eat is of great important for our health. A healthy diet plan can help us a lot as a preventive measure to avoid poor liver health, leading (among other troubles) to gallstones and potential gallbladder removal. More importantly, a healthy diet is also a primary curative measure for people who already went through an operation and had their gallbladder removed. Below you can find information on what to eat and whatnot, and why.

Protein

Meat, fish or eggs are all among the most important protein sources. Protein is necessary for the health of the body; however, overeating is not good for our liver. One of the major liver's responsibility is to metabolize complex proteins into basic particles and for the body to create its own proteins. When we eat plenty of protein-rich food, we can overload the liver, resulting (among others) in gallstones.

Excessive intake of protein can destroy the intestinal flora because it causes a decrease in the number of good microbes in the intestinal flora and increases the number of bad ones. This, in turn, weakens the detoxifying abilities of the body. In addition, too much protein food can acidify the body, which puts a strain on the liver again.

To put that into perspective, approx. 240 grams of meat (not pure protein) a day, especially if you consume it in smaller portions (some for lunch, some for dinner) will not cause any health problems. You should only avoid a larger daily protein intake.

Try eating lean meat, with as little amount of fat as possible. For example, chicken and turkey (boneless, skinless) and fish. Always try to buy fish low in mercury to burden your liver as little as possible. Some options include pollock, sardines, salmon, tilapia, herring, trout, oysters, shrimps, clams and crabs. On the contrary, avoid beef, pork and lamb, especially steaks or high-fat cuts of red meat and fatty meat substitutes.

In addition to meat, eggs and fish, you can gain protein from dairy products (such as milk, yogurt, cheese and others). However, you should limit the intake of fatty dairy, as it is hard to digest. Avoid eating full-fat yogurt, full-fat cheese, butter, lard, fatty sour cream or whipped cream, fatty sauce or gravies made with cream. Rather pick skim milk, fat-free yogurt and low-fat cheese or other dairy alternatives, such as vegan types of milk or yogurt (coconut and almond milk, etc.) and tofu. Vegan types of dairy are usually not rich in fat or sugar and contain a lot of fiber. They are also a great substitute for people who are lactose intolerant.

As regards the meat, eggs and dairy products, always choose products coming from a grass-fed or a free-range animal. These types of food include as little additives as possible or even no additives at all. Such food is usually ecological, organic and animal friendly. On the contrary, the meat coming from conventional and mass bread animals will burden the liver with residues of hormones, antibiotics and pesticides. The same applies to dairy products: raw organic milk and other organic dairy products have not suffered pasteurization, homogenization and consequently do not carry a bunch of toxins into our livers.

Make sure you do not eat highly processed meat substitutes, such as baloney, salami, sausages, fatty pates and others. Processed food includes unhealthy ingredients such as artificial colorings, flavorings, preservatives, and other industrial additives, as well as unhealthy omega 6 fatty acids, which are no good for you, as will be discussed below.

Carbohydrates

The liver and gallbladder are usually burdened by eating foods full of simple carbohydrates and fiber-poor foods. Such food directly acidifies the body and thus burdens the liver. It is high in sugar as well as calories, it therefore poses a great challenge to the body since it has trouble processing the excess glucose, which is released from these foods in large quantities and absorbed into the blood.

The body cannot consume a lot of glucose on a regular basis, so the liver has to process it into triglycerides. These, in turn, are stored in fat stores around the hips as well as in the liver. When the liver becomes too fatty as a result, it is difficult to perform well. That is when the disease is likely to occur. Make sure to limit an intake of simple carbohydrates, for example, white bread, pasta, cakes, pastries, and cookies made out of white flour.

Not all carbs are bad for your body if you choose the right sources. There are many health benefits for you and carbs are also a great energy source. So, focus on complex carbohydrates. For example, vegetables, sweet potatoes, oats, berries, and legumes are all great carbohydrate options. Other complex carbohydrate options include flakes, bran and full-grain flour products.

Fat

You should focus on healthy sources of fat such as fish, lean meat (skinless chicken or turkey), eggs, nuts, coconuts, olive oil and other unrefined and cold press vegetable oils (avocado oil, peanut oil, coconut oil, etc.).

You should be aware of the following facts about fat. Healthy fat is rich in omega-3 fatty acids. It can be found in nuts, fish, butter along with its better version: ghee butter, olives and avocados.

On the other hand, unhealthy fat can be found in margarine, heavily processed food and oils (such as chips, sweets, fast foods, etc.) and fatty meat (fatty parts of pork, beef, lamb, etc.). Some of the oils you should avoid, since they are nowadays highly processed and not cold-pressed, are canola, soybean, sunflower, and corn oil.

Food, reach in omega-6 fatty acids is heavy on your gastrointestinal tract as it is harder to digest and is, in general, harmful to your body. The consumption of larger quantities of unhealthy fat over long periods of time usually causes chronic inflammation and high cholesterol levels. This impacts your weight, but more importantly, your heart and liver health. Every person should avoid damaging the liver by eating fatty foods, especially those that have gallstones troubles or have just had their gallbladder removed.

On the contrary, eating healthy fat (omega-3 fatty acids) has no harmful effect on your body and can even positively affect your health by increasing the healthy cholesterol levels in your blood and helping you with the absorption of vitamins A, K and other fat-soluble vitamins.

Fruit and vegetable

Especially if you are recovering from gallbladder removal surgery, you will need nutritious, fiber-full food on your menu. This means you should include to your daily menu plan as much nutrient-dense fruits and vegetables as possible.

Food and vegetable are in general a great source of fiber vitamins and minerals. They help your body tremendously in recovery. Even if you did not go through the surgery yourself, eating fiber-full foods can boost your energy levels and improve your overall health.

Among the vegetable, it's recommended to eat cauliflower, cabbage, Brussels sprouts, broccoli, spinach, carrot, kale, tomatoes, sweet potatoes.

You can either eat the veggies raw or peel and cook them for easier digestion.

Among the fruits to enjoy are citruses (oranges, limes, lemons, etc.), avocadoes, blueberries, blackberries, raspberries and other berries, apples, applesauce, pears, plums and prunes, and of course, bananas. However, if you feel like you have digestion troubles, you might consider taking the peels off or cooking fruit prior to consumption.

Fiber

Fiber is known to improve your digestion in the absence of concentrated bile, which would otherwise come from your gallbladder. Similar to protein, you should not overeat it as it might cause gas and constipation.

Among the most fibrous food, you can eat legumes, such as peas, lentils, or beans. In addition, you can also eat potatoes (with or without skin), oats, barley, whole grain bread, pasta, rice or cereal, nuts (especially chia, poppy seeds, and other nuts or seeds).

Above listed sources of fiber are full of nutrients, such as calcium, B vitamins, and omega-3 fatty acids and are therefore very healthy for your body.

Sweets, Coffee and Alcohol

Sugar (including sweetened beverages, sweets, pastries, etc.), unrefined or not, should usually be avoided as it slows down metabolism, is hard to digest and can cause constipation. It can be used, though, in smaller quantities.

Sugar can cause addiction over time, moreover eating sugary foods leaves cravings throughout the day and can cause weight gain, binge eating and low energy levels. It is also linked to heart and liver diseases. A good option is to use natural and healthier sweeteners instead of raw sugar, like honey.

Among unsuitable products to consume is also alcohol. Similar to sugar and industrially processed food, it slows down your metabolism and could cause constipation. In addition, some types of alcohol are full of carbohydrates (among others, beer), and some are full of sugar (sweet vines, sweet liqueurs, etc.). This does not mean that you can't enjoy a glass of dry wine then and there. Just try to limit the quantities to a minimum.

Last but not least, caffeine. It contains different acids. As your stomach already makes acids itself, drinking a lot of coffee (or drinks and food, which include caffein) might encourage your stomach to make even more acid, resulting in stomach pain or discomfort. It is advisable to limit or (if possible) completely avoid all beverages and foods containing caffeine, such as coffee, soda, energy drinks and desserts and snacks which include caffeine.

TIPS AND TRICKS AND HOW TO USE THIS BOOK

In the beginning, diet adjustments might seem hard work to you, depending on what your everyday diet was before the gallbladder troubles. It might be especially hard for people who ate a lot of white bread, sweets and fast foods and did not cook a lot themselves.

Here are some tips and tricks for dieting:

- If you just had your surgery, don't start with solid foods right away. It is recommended to eat only liquid and easy to digest food for the first few days to ease your digestion and prevent any digestive issues;
- When introducing new foods after the surgery, be patient, try very small amounts first, and gradually increase it, if it does not cause you any symptoms;

- It is advisable to eat several smaller meals a day – if you manage, you can make 4-6 meals. If your gallbladder is removed, your liver needs time to adjust to a new digestion method so by eating small and often, you will help unburden your liver and ease the digestion;
- You shouldn't be eating more than 3 grams of fat per meal. Eating large amounts of fatty food at once can cause gas and bloating;
- Always have nutrient dense, low-fat, high-protein snacks on hand, such as unsweetened cereal bars, a protein bar, bananas or other fruit or a smoothie on the go. This way you won't be tempted to eat fast food or high fat snacks if you get hungry throughout the day. In addition, you won't be overeating during your next meal as you already calmed you stomach down with some food;
- Don't do any strenuous activity after eating, give your digestions system some time. As such activity may increase the risk of indigestion. However, you should not lay down in front of the TV or go for an afternoon snooze – a short walk is recommended, as it increases your digestion and stomach emptying;
- Try to drink sufficient amounts of water. You have to keep your body and your digestive system well hydrated so that the food would fall through easier;
- Exercise! It can fasten up your digestion and improve your health and fitness.

All in all, people are different. That is why you may experience different symptoms from day to day, depending on how you feel, how much sleep did you get, if you got enough liquid, etc. If you feel like your symptoms are severe or have worsened, try to stick with liquid food for some time to see if there is some improvement.

The recipes in this book are divided into four chapters: appetizer recipes, main meal recipes, dessert recipes and smoothies and drinks.

In addition, we included a bonus chapter at the end of the recipe book: recovery recipes! Recovery recipes are purposed for all who just had their surgery done or are experiencing severe symptoms. This chapter includes low or no-fat liquid food that is easy to digest to help cure your liver. In case your symptoms worsen over time, you can always come back to this liquid diet for a day or two to help your liver out.

At the end of the book, there is a 4-Week diet plan to ease you the path of planning meals and dieting.

The varieties of food in this book come with different tastes. Some are salty and sweet, while others are bitter and bland. If you do not tolerate certain spices presented in the recipes, feel free to skip or change them with something you like. The same applies to fruit and veggies – change them however you like. The sweeteners are always optional. You can skip them if you already had enough sugar for one day already. When choosing rice, flour or pasta, always choose whole grain. And of course, if you are lactose intolerant, you can replace animal based dairy products with vegan types of dairy. Most of all, have fun while cooking!

After a time, you will see that the recovery diet presented in this book is actually very healthy and fulfilling and might not be used only during the recovery phase but can be a long-term diet plan for you and your family. Nonetheless, you have to sustain a healthy liver until the end of your life in order to prevent potential disease, not necessarily limited to gallstones only.

Creating an ideal dietary plan doesn't come cheap. You have to invest in a lot of work while enjoying the journey!

APPETIZER RECIPES

Banana Walnut Pancakes

| Prep time: 10 min | Cook time: 5 min | Servings: 2 |

Ingredients

- 1 large banana
- 2 medium eggs, beaten
- *pinch of baking powder*
- *splash of vanilla extract*
- 1 tsp oil
- ¼ cup walnuts, roughly chopped
- ½ cup blueberry

Instructions

- Grab a bowl. Mash banana with a fork.
- Add 2 beaten eggs, a pinch of baking powder and a pinch of vanilla extract.

- Heat a large non-stick skillet or pancake over medium heat and brush with ½ tsp of oil.
- With half the batter, pour two pancakes into the pan, cook 1 to 2 minutes per side, then pour onto a plate. Repeat the process with another half tsp of oil and the rest of the dough.
- Top pancakes with walnuts and blueberries.

NUTRITION FACTS (PER SERVING)

Calories	267	
Total Fat	16.2g	21%
Saturated Fat	2.3g	11%
Cholesterol	164mg	55%
Sodium	63mg	3%
Total Carbohydrate	23.1g	8%
Dietary Fiber	3.7g	13%
Total Sugars	12.7g	
Protein	10.3g	

Tips: Banana pancakes will keep in the refrigerator for 4 to 5 days when stored in an airtight container.

Barley Oats Granola with Almond

| Prep time: 5 min | Cook time: 30 min | Servings: 12 |

Ingredients

- *1 cup rolled oats*
- *½ cup barley uncooked*
- *½ cup almond chopped*
- *¼ cup chia seeds*
- *⅛ tsp salt*
- *3 tbsp coconut oil melted*
- *3 tbsp stevia*
- *1 tsp pure vanilla extract*
- *¼ cup coconut flakes unsweetened*

Instructions

- Preheat the oven to 325 degrees F and line the baking sheet with parchment paper or a silicone mat.

- In a medium bowl, add the oats, barley, almond, chia seeds and salt. Stir to combine. Add the oil, stevia and vanilla extract. Mix well. Spread on the baking sheet.
- Bake on a third rack from the bottom for 25 minutes, sprinkle with coconut flakes and cook for another 5 minutes.
- Take the barley granola out of the oven, let it cool completely (do not touch it), then break it into pieces.

NUTRITION FACTS (PER SERVING)

Calories	137	
Total Fat	6.7g	9%
Saturated Fat	3.6g	18%
Cholesterol	0mg	0%
Sodium	26mg	1%
Total Carbohydrate	16.9g	6%
Dietary Fiber	2.9g	10%
Total Sugars	4.8g	
Protein	2.9g	

Tips: The right combination of fiber, protein, and carbohydrates makes barley a great post-workout snack.

Quinoa Coconut Chocolate Muffins

| Prep time: 5 min | Cook time: 30 min | Servings: 12 |

Ingredients

- *2 cups cooked quinoa*
- *2 large eggs*
- *½ cup coconut milk*
- *¼ cup applesauce unsweetened*
- *¼ cup coconut oil melted*
- *¼ cup honey*
- *½ cup cacao powder*
- *1 tsp pure vanilla extract*
- *1 tsp baking powder*
- *¼ tsp pink salt*
- *1 cup coconut flour*
- *½ cup coconut flakes unsweetened*
- *¼ cup chocolate chips*

Instructions

- Preheat the oven to 375 degrees F and line the muffin pan with a liner or use a silicone muffin pan.
- Beat the eggs in a large bowl.
- Add the coconut milk, applesauce, coconut oil, honey, cocoa powder, vanilla extract, baking powder and salt; easy to combine. Add chilled quinoa, coconut flour, coconut flakes and chocolate chips; mix well to combine.
- Divide the dough into 12 openings with a large ice cream scoop.
- Bake for 20 minutes, then let sit for 15 minutes to cool down.

NUTRITION FACTS (PER SERVING)		
Calories	230	
Total Fat	10.5g	13%
Saturated Fat	7.3g	36%
Cholesterol	32mg	11%
Sodium	29mg	1%
Total Carbohydrate	30.1g	11%
Dietary Fiber	3.9g	14%
Total Sugars	8.3g	
Protein	6.4g	

Tips: Store in a chilled and dry place for up to 4 days or freeze up to 3 months.

Crab, Dill Fritters

| Prep time: 5 min | Cook time: 20 min | Servings: 4 |

Ingredients

- *Approx. 16 ounces of crab meat*
- *2 egg whites*
- *3 tbsp reduced-fat Greek yogurt*
- *1 cup cauliflower rice (grated cauliflower)*
- *1 tbsp lemon juice*
- *2 tsp Dijon mustard*
- *2 tsp fresh dill*
- *½ tsp Old Bay seasoning*
- *½ cup Panko bread crumbs*

Instructions

- Set the oven to 350 degrees F.

- Combine the crab meat, Greek yoghurt, egg white, mustard, cauliflower rice, dill, lemon juice, and other spices in a bowl.
- Mix well. Weigh 4 ounces for each crab cake.
- In a separate bowl, toss each cake with the panko breadcrumbs to form a crust. Continue the process until all the crab cakes are coated with panko crumbs.
- After coating, place the crab cakes on a baking sheet.
- Bake for 20 minutes or until cakes are golden brown.

NUTRITION FACTS (PER SERVING)

Calories	127	
Total Fat	6.2g	8%
Saturated Fat	1g	5%
Cholesterol	9mg	3%
Sodium	350mg	15%
Total Carbohydrate	12g	4%
Dietary Fiber	0.8g	3%
Total Sugars	1.7g	
Protein	5.9g	

Tips: Crabs are a good source of protein, which is playing an important role in building and maintaining muscle. They are also rich in vitamin B12 and selenium.

Buckwheat Strawberry Pancakes

| Prep time: 10 min | Cook time: 20 min | Servings: 4 |

Ingredients

- *2 egg whites*
- *1 tbsp coconut oil*
- *½ cup coconut milk*
- *½ cup coconut flour*
- *½ cup buckwheat flour*
- *½ cup almond flour*
- *1 tbsp baking powder*
- *1 tbsp coconut sugar*
- *½ cup sparkling water*
- *3 cups sliced fresh strawberries*

Instructions

- In a small bowl, whisk together the egg whites, coconut oil and coconut milk.
- In another bowl, combine the flours, baking powder and coconut sugar. Add sparkling water and egg, oil and milk mixture and stir for a couple minutes.
- Place a non-stick frying pan over medium heat. When a drop of water sizzles as it hits the pan, spoon ½ cup pancake batter into the pan.
- Bale a pancake for approx. 2 min on each side. The bottoms of the pancake should be brown and bubbly. Repeat with the remaining pancake batter.
- Transfer the pancakes to individual plates. Top each with ½ cup sliced strawberries and serve immediately.

NUTRITION FACTS (PER SERVING)

Calories	143	
Total Fat	7.8g	10%
Saturated Fat	6.4g	32%
Cholesterol	0mg	0%
Sodium	21mg	1%
Total Carbohydrate	17.6g	6%
Dietary Fiber	3.4g	12%
Total Sugars	6.6g	
Protein	3.6g	

Tips: Buckwheat is a very nutritious whole grain that many people consider a superfood. It can improve heart health, promote weight loss, and help treat diabetes, among others.

Tangy Lime-Garlic Kale Shrimps

| Prep time: 10 min | Cook time: 10 min | Servings: 4 |

Ingredients

- 16 large shrimps - peeled, deveined, and tails on, or more to taste
- 3 cloves garlic (minced)
- 1 tsp crushed red pepper (more if desired)
- 2 tsp seafood seasoning or to taste
- salt and ground black pepper to taste
- 2 tbsp lime juice
- 3 tbsp chopped fresh parsley
- 3 tsp lime zest
- 1 cup chopped kale

Instructions

- Heat a large pan over medium-low heat for about 3 minutes. Add shrimps, garlic and crushed red pepper all at once and stir.

Add seafood seasoning, salt and black pepper. Mix everything together.
- Cook over medium heat, approx. 5 minutes, until the shrimp are cooked through.
- Add kale and cook for 2 min, then add the lime juice to the pot and stir again.
- Reduce the heat to low. Add the parsley and lime zest. Transfer only the shrimps and kale to a serving dish.

NUTRITION FACTS (PER SERVING)

Calories	293	
Total Fat	3.2g	4%
Saturated Fat	0.8g	4%
Cholesterol	553mg	184%
Sodium	707mg	31%
Total Carbohydrate	3.3g	1%
Dietary Fiber	0.5g	2%
Total Sugars	0.5g	
Protein	59.7g	

Tips: Shrimps have a variety of health benefits. They are rich in various vitamins and minerals and are a rich source of protein.

Apple Muffins with Cinnamon

| Prep time: 10 min | Cook time: 25 min | Servings: 16 |

Ingredients

- *1 cup non-fat plain sour cream*
- *2 eggs*
- *2 tbsp coconut oil*
- *2 tsp vanilla extract*
- *1 cup almond flour*
- *1 cup honey*
- *¾ cup milled oats*
- *¼ cup flaxseed meal*
- *2 tsp cinnamon*
- *¼ tsp nutmeg*
- *1 ½ tsp baking powder*
- *½ tsp salt*

- *2 medium peeled and chopped apples*

Instructions

- Preheat oven to 350 F and line the muffin pan with a liner or use a silicone muffin pan.
- Combine sour cream, eggs, oil and vanilla in a bowl.
- In a bowl, combine flour, oats, 1 cup honey, flax seeds, cinnamon, nutmeg, baking powder and salt. Turn on the blender at low speed.
- Add in the dry ingredients.
- Stir until everything is well combined. The dough should be lumpy. Work in the apples with a spatula.
- Fill the muffin pan with about ¼ cup of batter into each muffin space.
- Bake for about 22 minutes or until the top is golden and the toothpick comes out clean when you insert it.

NUTRITION FACTS (PER SERVING)		
Calories	187	
Total Fat	3.9g	9%
Saturated Fat	2.1g	10%
Cholesterol	21mg	7%
Sodium	94mg	4%
Total Carbohydrate	29.4g	11%
Dietary Fiber	3g	11%
Total Sugars	21.3g	
Protein	4.6g	

Tips: Apples with skins contain more vitamins A, C and K, 20% more calcium and up to 19% more potassium, compared to a peeled apple.

Millet Barley Pancakes

| Prep time: 10 min | Cook time: 25 min | Servings: 9 |

Ingredients

- *1 cup whole-wheat flour*
- *¼ cup millet flour*
- *½ cup barley flour*
- *2 tbsp flaxseed flour*
- *¼ cup rolled oats*
- *1 ½ tbsp baking powder*
- *3 tbsp maple syrup*
- *1 tbsp oil*
- *2 ¼ cups almond milk*
- *3 large egg whites, beaten*

Instructions

- Mix the dry ingredients in a bowl.
- In another bowl, combine the wet ingredients: maple syrup, oil, almond milk and whipped egg white. Add the egg mixture to the dry ingredients. Stir until everything is well combined.
- Put the dough in the refrigerator. Let it sit for 20-30 minutes.
- Put a baking sheet in the oven and heat it to 22 ° C.
- Set a saucepan over medium heat. Pour in about ¼ cup of batter to make a pancake. Cook for about 2 min on each side, or until the edges of the pancake appear a bit dry. Flip around and cook until on the other side, until brown. Transfer the pancakes to a baking sheet and in the oven to keep them warm. Repeat with the rest of the dough.
- To serve, garnish the pancakes with fresh fruit or a light coating of powdered sugar.

NUTRITION FACTS (PER SERVING)

Calories	287	
Total Fat	4g	22%
Saturated Fat	13g	65%
Cholesterol	0mg	0%
Sodium	24mg	1%
Total Carbohydrate	30.8g	11%
Dietary Fiber	3.6g	13%
Total Sugars	6.2g	
Protein	5.9g	

Tips: Whole grains have lots of health benefits. They lower cholesterol levels and help cure chronic inflammation, which is linked to cancer and heart disease.

Roasted Potatoes with Garlic and Parsley and Rosemary

| Prep time: 10 min | Cook time: 25 min | Servings: 4 |

Ingredients

- ¾ pound small potatoes
- 4 garlic cloves
- 2 tsp coconut oil
- 2 tsp chopped fresh rosemary
- ⅛ tsp salt
- ¼ tsp ground black pepper
- 2 tsp butter
- 2 tbsp chopped fresh parsley

Instructions

- Preheat oven to 400 F.
- Lay a large baking dish with parchment paper.

- To a large bowl, add the whole potatoes, garlic cloves, coconut oil, rosemary, salt and pepper. Mix until the potatoes are coated with oil and spices.
- Place the potatoes on the prepared baking dish, then cover and bake for 20-25 minutes.
- Remove the lid or foil. Flip the potatoes and cook them, uncovered, until the potatoes are tender and lightly browned (about 25 minutes).
- Put in a bowl and mix with butter. Sprinkle with parsley and serve.

NUTRITION FACTS (PER SERVING)

Calories	103	
Total Fat	4.4g	6%
Saturated Fat	3.2g	16%
Cholesterol	5mg	2%
Sodium	94mg	4%
Total Carbohydrate	15.1g	5%
Dietary Fiber	1.9g	7%
Total Sugars	0.9g	
Protein	1.9g	

<u>*Tips: Potatoes are a great source of fiber that can help you lose weight by keeping you fuller for longer. Fiber can help prevent heart disease by controlling cholesterol and blood sugar levels.*</u>

Mixed Flour Banana Bread

| Prep time: 10 min | Cook time: 60 min | Servings: 14 |

Ingredients

- ½ cup brown rice flour
- ½ cup amaranth flour
- ½ cup tapioca flour
- ½ cup millet flour
- ½ cup quinoa flour
- 1 tsp baking soda
- ½ tsp baking powder
- ⅛ tsp salt
- ¾ cup egg white
- 2 tbsp coconut oil
- ½ cup honey
- 2 cups mashed banana

Instructions

- Preheat the oven to 350 F. Prepare a 5 x 9-inch loaf pan by spraying it lightly with cooking spray. Sprinkle with a little flour. Put aside.
- Use a bowl to combine all dry ingredients (live out the sugar).
- In another bowl, combine the egg, oil, honey and mashed banana. Mix well.
- Put the wet and dry mixtures together and stir, until well combined. Pour into a loaf pan. Bake for 50 to 60 minutes.
- Take the bread out of the oven and let it cool for a bit.
- Slice it and serve.

NUTRITION FACTS (PER SERVING)

Calories	152	
Total Fat	2.7g	3%
Saturated Fat	1.6g	8%
Cholesterol	0mg	0%
Sodium	114mg	5%
Total Carbohydrate	29.3g	11%
Dietary Fiber	2g	7%
Total Sugars	11.2g	
Protein	3.7g	

Tips: Bananas are one of the famous fruits in the world. They are filled with lots of important nutrients.

Grilled Tangy and Sweet Pineapple

| Prep time: 10 min | Cook time: 60 min | Servings: 14 |

Ingredients

- *4 tbsp maple syrup*
- *2 tbsp coconut oil*
- *2 tbsp fresh lemon juice*
- *1 tsp ground cinnamon*
- *1 tsp nutmeg*
- *2 firm, ripe pineapple*
- *16 skewers (metal or wooden)*
- *2 tbsp grated lemon zest*

Instructions

- Build a hot fire on a charcoal grill or heat a gas grill or rotisserie (grill). Lightly coat with cooking spray away from heat source. Place the grill 4 to 6 inches from the heat source.
- For the marinade, mix and whisk the maple syrup, coconut oil, lemon juice, cinnamon and nutmeg in a small bowl. Put aside.
- Cut off the crown of the leaves and the base of the pineapple. Remove the skin with the sharp knife.
- Lay the pineapple on its side. Line up the blade of the knife with the diagonal rows of eyes and use a spiral pattern to cut a shallow groove around the pineapple to remove all of the eyes. Hold the peeled pineapple vertically and cut it in half lengthwise.
- Place each cut side of pineapple halfway and cut lengthwise into four long wedges. Cut the core. Cut each quarter into three pieces crosswise. Thread the three pieces of pineapple onto each skewer.
- Lightly brush the pineapple with the marinade. Broil, turn once and brush the remaining marinade once or twice until tender and golden, about 5 minutes per side. Remove and place on a platter or individual serving plates.
- If desired, brush with rum and sprinkle with lemon zest. Serve hot or warm.

NUTRITION FACTS (PER SERVING)		
Calories	40	
Total Fat	1.8g	2%
Saturated Fat	1.6g	8%
Cholesterol	0mg	0%
Sodium	1mg	0%
Total Carbohydrate	6.5g	2%
Dietary Fiber	0.5g	2%
Total Sugars	5.1g	
Protein	0.2g	

Tips: Eating a few slices of fresh pineapple every day can help protect your body from harmful free radicals and disease, aid your digestion by cleansing the body's organs and blood, increasing your energy intake and boosting metabolism, your hair, your skin, etc. your nails and teeth and keep you healthy, and that's it!

Breakfast Farro Porridge

| Prep time: 5 min | Cook time: 15 min | Servings: 8 |

Ingredients

- 8 cups almond milk
- 2 cup Farro
- ½ cup dried cherries
- ¼ tsp salt
- ½ cup dried peaches, coarsely chopped (2 oz)
- ⅓ cup sliced walnuts

Instructions

- In a medium saucepan, combine Farro, dried cherries, almond milk, dried cherries and salt. Bring to a boil.
- Reduce the heat to medium. Cook while stirring frequently, until the Farro is tender about (10 to 15 minutes).

- Divide the hot porridge among 8 bowls; Garnish with peaches and walnuts.

NUTRITION FACTS (PER SERVING)

Calories	367	
Total Fat	32.1g	41%
Saturated Fat	25.6g	128%
Cholesterol	0mg	0%
Sodium	93mg	4%
Total Carbohydrate	18.6g	7%
Dietary Fiber	4.9g	18%
Total Sugars	5g	
Protein	5.9g	

Tips: Farro is an excellent source of fiber, iron, protein, and magnesium.

Stuffed Mushrooms with Herbs

| Prep time: 10 min | Cook time: 60 min | Servings: 10 |

Ingredients

- *10 mushrooms (without stems)*

Topping:

- *¾ cup cornflakes (crushed)*
- *2 tbsp melted coconut oil*
- *1,5 tbsp fresh parsley*

Filling:

- *1 cup fresh basil leaves*
- *2 tbsp grated Parmesan cheese*
- *1 tsp pine nuts*
- *1 tsp pumpkin seed*
- *1 tsp sunflower seeds*
- *1 tsp olive oil*

- *1 tsp minced garlic (or more to taste)*
- *1 tsp freshly squeezed lemon juice*
- *Pinch of salt*

Instructions

- Preheat oven to 350 F.
- Line a baking sheet with baking paper. Place mushrooms on a baking sheet, upside down.
- Combine the crushed cornflakes, coconut oil and chopped parsley in a small bowl, for the topping. Set aside.
- For the filling, place the basil, Parmesan, pumpkin seeds, sunflower seeds, pine nuts, olive oil, garlic, salt and lemon juice in a food processor. Process until well combined.
- Fill the mushroom caps with the filling and sprinkle each mushroom with about 1 tsp of topping.
- Bake for 10 or 15 minutes or until the mushrooms are golden brown.

NUTRITION FACTS (PER SERVING)

Calories	51	
Total Fat	2.9g	4%
Saturated Fat	0.9g	4%
Cholesterol	0mg	0%
Sodium	121mg	5%
Total Carbohydrate	5.4g	2%
Dietary Fiber	0.9g	3%
Total Sugars	0.5g	
Protein	1.5g	

Tips: Mushrooms are low in calories and a great source of fiber, protein, and antioxidants. They may also reduce the risk of Alzheimer's, heart disease, cancer, and diabetes.

Chicken Tenders with Pineapple

| Prep time: 20 min | Cook time: 10 min | Servings: 10 |

Ingredients

- 1 cup pineapple juice
- ½ cup honey
- ⅓ cup light soy sauce
- 2 pounds chicken breast strips
- skewers

Instructions

- In a small saucepan over medium heat, combine the pineapple juice, honey and soy sauce. Remove from heat just before cooking.
- Place the chicken fillets in a medium bowl. Cover with the pineapple marinade and store in the refrigerator for at least 30 minutes.

- Preheat the grill to medium heat. Thread the chicken lengthwise onto wooden skewers.
- Lightly grease the grill. Grill the chicken fillets for 5 minutes per side or until juices run clear.
- They cook quickly so watch them closely.

NUTRITION FACTS (PER SERVING)

Calories	99	
Total Fat	1g	1%
Saturated Fat	0.2g	1%
Cholesterol	7mg	2%
Sodium	300mg	13%
Total Carbohydrate	20.1g	7%
Dietary Fiber	0.1g	0%
Total Sugars	16.7g	
Protein	3.7g	

Tips: Chicken is very nutritious and a good source of protein. It can help with weight loss as it contains very little fat in comparison to some other meat opions.

Fresh Fruit Kebabs

| Prep time: 20 min | Cook time: 0 min | Servings: 2 |

Ingredients

- *6 ounces low-fat, sugar-free lemon yogurt*
- *1 tsp fresh lemon juice*
- *1 tsp lemon zest*
- *4 pineapple chunks (about ½ inch each)*
- *4 strawberries*
- *1 kiwi, peeled and quartered*
- *½ banana, cut into 4 ½-inch chunks*
- *4 red grapes*
- *4 apples, chunks*
- *1 melon, diced*
- *4 wooden skewers*

Instructions

- Combine yogurt, lemon juice and lemon zest in a small bowl. Cover and refrigerate until ready to serve.
- Put one piece of each fruit on the skewer. Repeat the process until there is no more fruit left.
- Serve with lemon and lime sauce.

NUTRITION FACTS (PER SERVING)

Calories	131	
Total Fat	0.5g	1%
Saturated Fat	0.1g	0%
Cholesterol	0mg	0%
Sodium	163mg	7%
Total Carbohydrate	32.2g	12%
Dietary Fiber	4.1g	15%
Total Sugars	22.4g	
Protein	2.3g	

Tips: Fruit is a good source of essential vitamins and minerals and is high in fiber. Fruits also offer a wide range of health-promoting antioxidants, including flavonoids.

Maple Syrup-Glazed Herbed Sweet Potatoes

| Prep time: 30 min | Cook time: 0 min | Servings: 8 |

Ingredients

- ¼ cup water
- 2 tbsp coconut sugar
- 2 tbsp maple syrup
- 1 tbsp coconut oil
- 2 pounds sweet potatoes
- Handful of chopped herbs

Instructions

- Preheat oven to 375 F. Coat a 9-by-13-inch baking dish with cooking spray or lay in parchment paper.
- For the sauce, put the water, coconut sugar, maple syrup and coconut oil in a small bowl. Beat until smooth.
- Peel and cut the sweet potatoes into thin pieces.

- Place some of the potato slices on the baking dish – less is more. Put the sauce on the sweet potatoes. Rotate them to cover them.
- Cover with a lid or aluminum foil and bake for about 45 minutes until tender. Flip the sweet potatoes once or twice to continue garnishing. Once tender, remove the lid and bake for about 15 minutes until the frosting is firm.
- Place on a platter and garnish with fresh herbs of choice, for example parsley, thyme, etc.
- Eat immediately.

NUTRITION FACTS (PER SERVING)

Calories	190	
Total Fat	2g	3%
Saturated Fat	1.5g	8%
Cholesterol	0mg	0%
Sodium	21mg	1%
Total Carbohydrate	41g	15%
Dietary Fiber	4.8g	17%
Total Sugars	4.9g	
Protein	2g	

Tips: A single sweet potato can contain 769% of the amount of vitamin A, you need to consume on a daily basis. Vitamin A is great for your skin and it strengthens the immune system.

Zucchini Chips with Parmesan Cheese

| Prep time: 5 min | Cook time: 10 min | Servings: 4 |

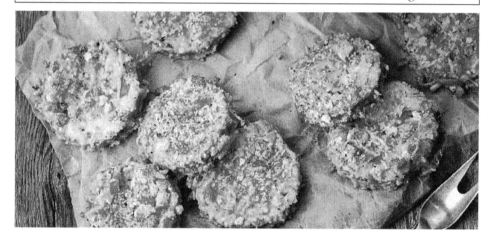

Ingredients

- 2 medium zucchinis, cut into ¼-inch slices
- ½ cup seasoned panko bread crumbs
- ⅛ tsp ground black pepper
- 2 tbsp grated Parmesan cheese
- 2 egg whites

Instructions

- Preheat the oven to 245 ° C.
- Combine breadcrumbs, pepper and Parmesan cheese in a small bowl. Put the egg whites in another dish.
- First, start dipping zucchinis into the egg whites, then coat them with breadcrumbs.

- Place them on a greased baking sheet.
- Bake in the oven for approx. 5 minutes, then flip them around and bake another 5 to 10 minutes until golden yellow and crisp.

NUTRITION FACTS (PER SERVING)

Calories	127	
Total Fat	4g	5%
Saturated Fat	2.3g	11%
Cholesterol	10mg	3%
Sodium	420mg	18%
Total Carbohydrate	14.2g	5%
Dietary Fiber	1.8g	7%
Total Sugars	2.7g	
Protein	9.6g	

Tips: Zucchini is rich in natural nutrients, vitamins C and A, potassium, folic acid, and fiber.

Grilled Spicy Sweet Potato with Garlic

| Prep time: 5 min | Cook time: 5 min | Servings: 4 |

Ingredients

- 1-pound peeled sweet potato
- ¼ cup chili sauce
- 1 tsp smoked paprika
- ½ tsp garlic powder
- ½ tsp onion powder
- ½ tsp chili powder (optional)
- ½ tsp ground cumin

Instructions

- Preheat a grill to medium-high heat and lightly grease it.

- Put potatoes in a bowl and add in paprika, chili sauce and chili powder, onion and powder and cumin.
- Toss around so that the potatoes are seasoned evenly.
- Using large tongs, place the sweet potatoes on the preheated grill and cook, 3 to 4 minutes, until they are pale pink on the outside and the meat in the center is no longer translucent.

NUTRITION FACTS (PER SERVING)

Calories	118	
Total Fat	1.4g	2%
Saturated Fat	0.4g	2%
Cholesterol	221mg	74%
Sodium	258mg	11%
Total Carbohydrate	1.1g	0%
Dietary Fiber	0.4g	1%
Total Sugars	0.3g	
Protein	24g	

Tips: Garlic is great for your health. It reduces risk factors like blood pressure, cholesterol, and heavy metal toxicity which can help people live longer. It is also a great source of nutrients and strengthens your immune system.

Potato Cauliflower Pancakes

| Prep time: 15 min | Cook time: 15 min | Servings: 4 |

Ingredients

- *6-8 red potatoes*
- *2 cups grated Cauliflower*
- *½ onion, shredded*
- *1 leek, chopped*
- *2 eggs*
- *3 tbsp almond flour*
- *½ tsp garlic powder*
- *½ tsp salt*
- *½ tsp ground black pepper*

Instructions

- Pill and smash potatoes.

- Combine them with cauliflower, onions, eggs, leek, almond flour, garlic powder, salt and black pepper in a bowl.
- Spray the skillet with cooking spray and put on medium heat.
- Place the potato mixture in the pan in large spoons and cook, 3 to 4 minutes, until the edges are dry and golden brown.
- Flip on the other side and cook for about 4 minutes or until golden brown. Repeat with the rest of the potato mixture.
- Enjoy!

NUTRITION FACTS (PER SERVING)		
Calories	165	
Total Fat	2.3g	3%
Saturated Fat	0.7g	3%
Cholesterol	82mg	27%
Sodium	331mg	14%
Total Carbohydrate	30.8g	11%
Dietary Fiber	2.3g	8%
Total Sugars	2.6g	
Protein	7.1g	

Tips: After mashing, soak the potatoes in cold water to prevent discoloration.

Carrot Parsnips Tzimmes with Parsley

| Prep time: 10 min | Cook time: 35 min | Servings: 6 |

Ingredients

- *1 tbsp olive oil*
- *1 ½ pounds carrots*
- *1-pound parsnips cut into ¼-inch rounds*
- *⅓ cup seedless golden raisins*
- *¼ cup freshly squeezed orange juice*
- *1 ½ tbsp maple syrup*
- *1 ½ tbsp coconut sugar*
- *A pinch of salt and pepper*
- *2 tbsp minced fresh parsley*

Instructions

- Over medium heat, heat the oil in a pen.
- Peeled the carrots and cut them into 1/4-inch rounds.

- Add carrots, parsnip raisins, orange juice, maple syrup, coconut sugar, salt and pepper; bring to a boil.
- Reduce the heat.
- Cover and simmer for about 20-25 minutes until the carrots are tender.
- Increase heat and cook until sauce thickens, about 5 minutes.
- Sprinkle with parsley before serving.

NUTRITION FACTS (PER SERVING)		
Calories	81	
Total Fat	2.5g	3%
Saturated Fat	0.3g	2%
Cholesterol	0mg	0%
Sodium	22mg	1%
Total Carbohydrate	14.7g	5%
Dietary Fiber	0.9g	3%
Total Sugars	8.5g	
Protein	0.7g	

Tips: Carrots are packed with beta-carotene, fiber, vitamin K1, potassium, and antioxidants.

Chia Seed Parfaits with Lime and Berries

| Prep time: 10 min | Cook time: 0 min | Servings: 8 |

Ingredients

- *4 cups coconut milk*
- *¼ cup coconut sugar*
- *4 tbsp lime juice*
- *4 tbsp grated lime zest*
- *4 tbsp chia seeds*
- *2 tsp vanilla extract*
- *2 cups fresh raspberries*
- *2 cups fresh blueberries*
- *2 cups strawberries*

Instructions

- Put the coconut milk, coconut sugar, lime juice, lime zest, chia seed, and vanilla extract in a pot.
- Layer half of the milk mixture into 8 custard cups. Top with half of the berries. Repeat layers.
- Serve immediately.

NUTRITION FACTS (PER SERVING)

Calories	405	
Total Fat	33.4g	43%
Saturated Fat	25.9g	129%
Cholesterol	0mg	0%
Sodium	24mg	1%
Total Carbohydrate	26.7g	10%
Dietary Fiber	11.3g	40%
Total Sugars	11.1g	
Protein	6.1g	

Tips: Chia seeds are packed with important nutrients. They are a rich source of omega-3 fatty acids, which are rich in antioxidants and contain fiber, iron and calcium.

Banana Quinoa

| Prep time: 15 min | Cook time: 0 min | Servings: 6 |

Ingredients

- *4 cups soy milk*
- *2 cups quinoa*
- *2 large ripe bananas, sliced*
- *2 tsp honey*
- *½ tsp ground nutmeg*

Instructions

- Put a saucepan on medium heat and add in the milk and bring to a boil.

- Add quinoa. Cook over medium heat for 1 to 2 minutes or until thickened, stirring occasionally.
- Add the banana, honey and nutmeg. Serve with more milk and nutmeg if desired.

NUTRITION FACTS (PER SERVING)

Calories	355	
Total Fat	6.5g	8%
Saturated Fat	0.8g	4%
Cholesterol	0mg	0%
Sodium	87mg	4%
Total Carbohydrate	61.7g	22%
Dietary Fiber	6.2g	22%
Total Sugars	16.6g	
Protein	13.9g	

Tips: The protein in soy milk is healthy, plant-based, and can help support healthy muscles and organs. Soy milk is high in omega-3 fatty acids, which are "healthy" fats that your body cannot make on its own.

Omelet with Brussels Sprouts & Asiago Cheese

| Prep time: 15 min | Cook time: 10 min | Servings: 2 |

Ingredients

- *1-½ cups fresh Brussels Sprouts, cut into pieces*
- *3 large eggs*
- *⅛ cup coconut milk*
- *¼ tsp salt*
- *⅛ tsp pepper*
- *⅙ cup grated Asiago cheese*
- *⅓ cup sliced pitted Greek olives*
- *1 tbsp coconut oil*
- *Shaved Asiago cheese and minced fresh basil*

Instructions

- Preheat the grill. Place the steamer basket in a large saucepan over 1 inch apart. Add some water. Place the Brussels Sprouts in the basket. Bring the water to a boil. Reduce heat to simmer.
- Steam, covered, 4 to 6 minutes or until soft and tender.
- Put milk in a bowl. Add the eggs, salt and pepper and wish together. Add the cooked Brussels Sprouts, grated cheese and olives.
- In a 10-inch refractory skillet, heat oil over medium heat; add the egg mixture. Cook uncovered for 7 to 10 minutes or until the eggs are set.
- Leave to rest for 5 minutes. Cut into quarters. Sprinkle with grated cheese and basil.

NUTRITION FACTS (PER SERVING)		
Calories	234	
Total Fat	19.1g	24%
Saturated Fat	11.9g	59%
Cholesterol	281mg	94%
Sodium	481mg	21%
Total Carbohydrate	5.8g	2%
Dietary Fiber	2.2g	8%
Total Sugars	2g	
Protein	11.9g	

Tips: Make sure the eggs you use are at room temperature before cooking. When you take the egg out of the fridge to make a good omelet, set it aside for a while. Cold eggs take longer to set.

Vegetable Scrambled Eggs

| Prep time: 15 min | Cook time: 10 min | Servings: 4 |

Ingredients

- 8 large eggs, lightly beaten
- ½ cup almond milk
- ½ cup chopped green pepper
- ¼ cup sliced green onions
- ½ cup kale chopped
- ½ cup green beans
- ¼ cup broccoli, chopped
- ¼ tsp salt
- ⅛ tsp pepper
- 1 small tomato, chopped and seeded

Instructions

- In a small bowl, mix together the eggs and milk.

- Add the green peppers, green onions, kale, green beans, broccoli, salt and pepper. Shape in a lightly greased saucepan.
- Cook over medium heat, stirring frequently, until eggs are almost ready, 2-3 minutes. Add the tomato.
- Cook until the eggs are set, stirring regularly.

NUTRITION FACTS (PER SERVING)		
Calories	231	
Total Fat	17.2g	22%
Saturated Fat	9.5g	47%
Cholesterol	372mg	124%
Sodium	301mg	13%
Total Carbohydrate	6.6g	2%
Dietary Fiber	2.1g	7%
Total Sugars	3.1g	
Protein	14.4g	

Tips: Adding the eggs directly to the pan and using a spoon or spatula will result in non-smooth, scratched scrambled eggs.

Sweet Potato Garlicky Omelet

| Prep time: 10 min | Cook time: 20 min | Servings: 8 |

Ingredients

- 4 medium sweet potatoes, peeled and diced
- 2 tbsp coconut oil
- ½ cup sliced green onions
- ½ cup leek, sliced
- ¼ cup minced fresh parsley
- ½ cup minced fresh basil
- 2 garlic cloves, minced
- 12 large eggs
- ¼ cup water
- ½ tsp salt
- ⅛ tsp pepper

Instructions

- In a skillet, cook the sweet potatoes in coconut oil over medium heat for 10 minutes or until golden brown, stirring occasionally.
- Add green onion, leek, parsley, basil and garlic; cook until tender. Reduce the heat to medium.
- Whisk the eggs, water, salt and pepper in a bowl. Pour over the sweet potato mixture.
- Cook covered for around 10 minutes.
- Cut into quarters and serve.

NUTRITION FACTS (PER SERVING)

Calories	233	
Total Fat	11g	14%
Saturated Fat	5.3g	27%
Cholesterol	279mg	93%
Sodium	263mg	11%
Total Carbohydrate	23.2g	8%
Dietary Fiber	3.5g	12%
Total Sugars	1.4g	
Protein	10.9g	

Tips: Sweet potatoes are an ample and natural source of beta-carotene and vitamin A. Vitamin A is playing an important role in helping the body fight infections and remain resistant to other infections.

Herb Frittatas with Zucchini and Tomato

| Prep time: 10 min | Cook time: 30 min | Servings: 6 |

Ingredients

- 6 large eggs
- ½ tsp salt
- ¼ tsp pepper
- 1-½ tbsp coconut oil
- 1 celery, chopped
- 1 tsp garlic powder
- 1 cup chopped zucchini
- ½ cup diced tomato
- ½ tbsp chopped fresh parsley
- ½ tbsp chopped fresh basil

- ½ tbsp chopped fresh oregano

Instructions

- Preheat the oven to 350 ° F. Brush a 6-cup non-stick muffin pan with cooking spray or lay in parchment paper.
- In a large bowl, beat the eggs with salt and pepper until well combined.
- Heat the coconut oil in a skillet. Fry celery until tender but not brown, 3 to 5 minutes. Add the garlic powder and sauté for a further minute. Add zucchini and tomato cook for 5 to 6 minutes. Remove the heat and let cool a bit.
- Beat vegetable mixture and herbs in eggs.
- Divide among 6 muffin bowls and bake 25 to 30 minutes; serve warm.

NUTRITION FACTS (PER SERVING)

Calories	101	
Total Fat	4.4g	9%
Saturated Fat	3.5g	18%
Cholesterol	186mg	62%
Sodium	272mg	12%
Total Carbohydrate	2.5g	1%
Dietary Fiber	0.7g	3%
Total Sugars	1.3g	
Protein	6.9g	

Tips: Eating herbs can help prevent and control heart disease, cancer, and diabetes. It can also help reduce blood clots and provide anti-inflammatory and anti-tumor properties.

MAIN MEALS

Ginger Tempeh and Vegetable Stir-Fry

| Prep time: 10 min | Cook time: 30 min | Servings: 6 |

Ingredients

- 1 block Tempeh
- ¾ cup Coconut aminos
- ½ cup lime juice
- 2 tbsp fresh ginger minced
- 4 tbsp coconut oil (or olive oil)
- 1 cup zucchini, chopped
- 1 cup cauliflower, chopped
- 2 parsnips, sliced
- 1 onion, chopped
- red bell pepper, sliced
- 1 cup asparagus, sliced
- 1 cup eggplant, sliced,

- 1 leek, sliced
- 1 cup cooked quinoa

Instructions

- Cut the tempeh into 1-inch cubes.
- In a large, shallow bowl, combine the coconut aminos, lime juice and ginger.
- Marinate the tempeh in this sauce for at least 1 hour. If you need to cook the quinoa, do so at this point.
- In a wok or large skillet, add the coconut oil and cook the zucchini, cauliflower, parsnips, onions, red peppers and tempeh over high heat, stirring frequently.
- Add the asparagus, eggplant, leek and tempeh marinade. Simmer a few more minutes. The vegetables should be tender but not mushy.

  Add the quinoa and cook until heated through and well combined. Serve and enjoy.

NUTRITION FACTS (PER SERVING)

Calories	441	
Total Fat	1.5g	24%
Saturated Fat	10.7g	53%
Cholesterol	0mg	0%
Sodium	146mg	6%
Total Carbohydrate	57.5g	21%
Dietary Fiber	8.7g	31%
Total Sugars	8.7g	
Protein	14.5g	

Tips: Leftover stir fry should be refrigerated in a covered container. You can simply put it in the microwave to reheat it and enjoy it for lunch or dinner the next day.

Grilled Turkey Teriyaki

Prep time: 15 min   Cook time: 20 min   Servings: 4

Ingredients

- *2 tbsp Coconut aminos*
- *1 tbsp apple cider vinegar*
- *1 tbsp minced fresh ginger root*
- *1 large clove garlic, minced*
- *4 (6 ounces) turkey breast*
- *1 tbsp olive oil*

Instructions

- Combine coconut aminos, apple cider vinegar, ginger and garlic in a shallow bowl. Put the turkey breast in the marinade and turn it over to coat it. Cover the plate and refrigerate for at least 30 to 45 minutes.

- Preheat the grill.
- Remove the breast out of the marinade.
- Discard any remaining liquid. Brush both sides of the meat with oil.
- Cook the turkey breast on the preheated grill, 10 to 15 minutes per side, until cooked through.
- Serve with herbs, rice or veggies of your choice.

NUTRITION FACTS (PER SERVING)

Calories	217	
Total Fat	6.3g	8%
Saturated Fat	1.1g	5%
Cholesterol	73mg	24%
Sodium	1735mg	75%
Total Carbohydrate	9.1g	3%
Dietary Fiber	0.9g	3%
Total Sugars	6g	
Protein	29.1g	

<u>*Tips: Turkey breast is a good source of B vitamins, including B3 (niacin), B6 (pyridoxine) and B12 (cobalamin).*</u>

Sautéed Turkey and Cabbage

| Prep time: 20 min | Cook time: 20 min | Servings: 4 |

Ingredients

- *2 turkey breasts, skinless, boneless and sliced*
- *1 head of cabbage, shredded*
- *2 carrots, shredded*
- *3 tbsp paprika*
- *3 tomatoes, pureed*
- *1 cup chicken stock*
- *2 tbsp coconut oil*
- *sea salt and freshly ground black pepper*

Instructions

- Heath the coconut oil in a skillet over medium heat.

- Cook the turkey slices until golden brown on each side.
- When you are almost done, add the shredded cabbage and carrots to the pan and cook, stirring, for 4-5 minutes.
- Add the tomatoes, chicken broth, paprika and season to taste.
- Stir the content well, then bring it to a boil.
- Lower the heat and simmer for 10 to 12 minutes to make sure the turkey is cooked through.
- Remove from the heat and serve hot.

NUTRITION FACTS (PER SERVING)

Calories	172	
Total Fat	8.3g	11%
Saturated Fat	6.2g	31%
Cholesterol	9mg	3%
Sodium	469mg	20%
Total Carbohydrate	20.9g	8%
Dietary Fiber	8.4g	30%
Total Sugars	11.1g	
Protein	7.9g	

Tips: Cabbage contains a lot of nutrients and is a great side dish to poultry.

Ginger Glazed Tuna

| Prep time: 5 min | Cook time: 15 min | Servings: 2 |

Ingredients

- *1-½ tbsp maple syrup*
- *1-½ tbsp coconut aminos*
- *1-½ tbsp apple cider vinegar*
- *½ tsp grated fresh ginger root*
- *½ tsp garlic powder*
- *1 tsp coconut oil*
- *2 (6 ounces) tuna fillets*
- *salt and pepper to taste*
- *½ tbsp avocado oil*

Instructions

- In a small glass bowl, combine the maple syrup, coconut aminos, apple cider vinegar, ginger, garlic powder and coconut oil.

- Place the fillets on a plate and sprinkle salt and pepper. Cover to marinate and refrigerate for 20 minutes.
- Heath the oil in a skillet, over medium heat. Remove the fish from the plate and keep the marinade. Bake the fish on a pan for 4 to 6 minutes per side, turning it just once, until tender.
- Place the steaks on a platter. Keep them warm.
- Heath the remaining marinade into the skillet, over medium heat until the mixture is evenly reduced to a glaze.
- Pour it over the fillets and serve immediately. If desired, serve with some brown rice.

NUTRITION FACTS (PER SERVING)

Calories	88	
Total Fat	2.8g	4%
Saturated Fat	0.6g	3%
Cholesterol	9mg	3%
Sodium	16mg	1%
Total Carbohydrate	7.6g	3%
Dietary Fiber	0.2g	1%
Total Sugars	6.2g	
Protein	7.7g	

Tips: The high levels of omega-3 in tuna can help reduce the levels of omega-6 and LDL cholesterol that can build up in the arteries of the heart. Studies have shown that consuming more omega-3 fatty acids is linked to reduced rates of cardiovascular disease, including heart attacks.

Egg Fried Quinoa

| Prep time: 5 min | Cook time: 15 min | Servings: 2 |

Ingredients

- 1 cup water
- ¼ tsp salt
- 1 tbsp coconut aminos
- ½ cup uncooked quinoa
- ½ tsp vegetable oil
- ½ onion, finely chopped
- ½ cup green beans
- ½ cup green peas
- ½ cup carrot, sliced
- ¼ cup corn
- 1 egg, lightly beaten
- ¼ tsp ground black pepper

Instructions

- Bring the water, salt and coconut aminos to a boil in a saucepan. Add the quinoa and stir. Remove from the heat.
- Cover and let sit for 5 minutes.
- Heat the oil in a medium skillet or wok over medium heat. Sauté the onions and green beans, green peas, carrot, corn for 2 to 3 minutes. Pour in the egg and fry it for 2 minutes, stirring the egg as it cooks.
- Add the cooked quinoa, mix well and sprinkle with pepper.

NUTRITION FACTS (PER SERVING)

Calories	275	
Total Fat	6.4g	8%
Saturated Fat	1.3g	6%
Cholesterol	82mg	27%
Sodium	354mg	15%
Total Carbohydrate	43.7g	16%
Dietary Fiber	7.6g	27%
Total Sugars	5.8g	
Protein	12.4g	

Tips: Quinoa is much higher in fiber than most grains. One study found 17 to 27 grams of fiber per cup (185 grams).

Garlic Turkey Breasts with Lemon

| Prep time: 10 min | Cook time: 25 min | Servings: 2 |

Ingredients

- *1 tsp garlic powder*
- *2 skinless, turkey breast halves*
- *salt and ground black pepper to taste*
- *½ cup chicken broth*
- *½ tbsp lemon juice*
- *1 tbsp chopped cilantro*

Instructions

- Place the nonstick skillet over low heat.

- Season the breast with garlic powder, salt and pepper and place it on a skillet. Cook over medium heat, 10 to 12 minutes, until golden brown on both sides.
- Add in the chicken broth. Bring to a boil, then reduce the heat to medium-low, add lemon juice and cover the pan and simmer for 10 to 15 minutes until the breast is no longer pink in the center.
- Place the breast on the serving platter and keep the liquid in the pan. Simmer the liquid for about 3 minutes until slightly reduced. Pour liquid over the breast.
- Garnish with fresh Cilantro.

NUTRITION FACTS (PER SERVING)

Calories	158	
Total Fat	4.7g	6%
Saturated Fat	1.7g	8%
Cholesterol	65mg	22%
Sodium	232mg	10%
Total Carbohydrate	1.4g	0%
Dietary Fiber	0.2g	1%
Total Sugars	0.6g	
Protein	26.5g	

Tips: turkey is a rich source of iron, magnesium, selenium, and omega-3 fatty acids.

Maple Syrup-Orange Glazed Salmon

| Prep time: 10 min | Cook time: 10 min | Servings: 6 |

Ingredients

- *1.5-pound salmon fillets*
- *1 cup asparagus*
- *4 tbsp orange zest*
- *2 tbsp maple syrup*
- *1 tbsp orange juice*
- *2 tsp yellow mustard*
- *1 tsp coconut oil*

- 1 tsp Coconut aminos
- ¼ tsp freshly ground black pepper
- 4 tbsp chopped fresh basil, or to taste

Instructions

- Place an oven rack 5 to 6 inches from the heat source and preheat the oven rack. Brush a pan with cooking spray (or lay in the parchment paper) and top with the salmon.
- Combine orange zest, maple syrup, orange juice, yellow mustard, coconut oil, coconut aminos and pepper in a small bowl. Mix well.
- Roast the salmon and asparagus in a preheated oven for 4 to 5 minutes. Spread half the maple syrup orange frosting on top and grill until fish flakes easily with a fork, another 4 to 5 minutes. Set the time according to the thickness of the fillets.
- Spread the rest of the glaze over the fillets. Garnish with basil.

NUTRITION FACTS (PER SERVING)		
Calories	187	
Total Fat	2.3g	3%
Saturated Fat	0.8g	4%
Cholesterol	67mg	22%
Sodium	119mg	5%
Total Carbohydrate	17.7g	6%
Dietary Fiber	0.8g	3%
Total Sugars	15.1g	
Protein	25.1g	

Tips: If you grill salmon fillets in the oven, you will end up with a nice, juicy fish that does not require constant attention.

Garlicky Barley and Pinto Beans

| Prep time: 15 min | Cook time: 35 min | Servings: 6 |

Ingredients

- ½ tsp coconut oil
- ½ onion, chopped
- 1 tsp garlic powder
- ½ cup barley
- ½ cup vegetable broth
- ½ cup water
- ½ tsp ground cumin
- ¼ tsp cayenne pepper
- salt and ground black pepper to taste
- ½ cup green peas
- ½ cup broccoli
- 1(15 ounces) cans pinto beans, rinsed and drained

- ¼ cup chopped fresh cilantro

Instructions

- Heat oil in a saucepan over medium heat; cook and stir onion and garlic powder until lightly browned, about 10 minutes.
- Toss the barley with the onion mixture and top with the vegetable broth and water. Season with cumin, cayenne pepper, salt and pepper.
- Bring the mixture to a boil. Cover, reduce the heat and simmer, about 20 minutes, until the barley is tender and the liquid is absorbed.
- Add the green peas, broccoli, carrot to the pot and simmer for about 5 minutes until heated through. Stir in the pinto beans and cilantro and serve.

NUTRITION FACTS (PER SERVING)

Calories	189	
Total Fat	1.3g	2%
Saturated Fat	0.5g	2%
Cholesterol	0mg	0%
Sodium	55mg	2%
Total Carbohydrate	35.2g	13%
Dietary Fiber	8.9g	32%
Total Sugars	2.3g	
Protein	9.9g	

Tips: If you are using dry beans - cover cleaned dried beans with plenty of water (3 to 4 cups of water per cup of beans). Let them soak for at least 8 hours, preferably overnight, then drain and rinse before cooking.

Creamy Broccoli and Sweet Potato Soup

| Prep time: 20 min | Cook time: 35 min | Servings: 4 |

Ingredients

- ½ tbsp coconut oil
- ½ onion, coarsely chopped
- 2 large cloves garlic, coarsely chopped
- 2 broccoli florets and stalks chopped
- 1 cauliflower florets
- 1 big sweet potato
- ¼ leek root, coarsely chopped
- 2 cups vegetable stock
- 2 cups coconut milk

Instructions

- Heat the oil in a saucepan over medium heat.

- Add the onion and garlic and cook and stir for 10 to 15 minutes until translucent.
- Add the pilled and chopped sweet potatoes, broccoli florets, cauliflower florets, and leek. Stir until coated with oil. Top the vegetables with the vegetable broth and coconut milk; bring to a boil.
- Reduce heat and simmer, stirring occasionally, until the vegetables can bite easily with a fork, 20 to 25 minutes. Remove the soup from the heat.
- Don't fill a blender more than half full with liquid and vegetables. Cover and hold the lid. Pulse several times before bringing the blender to full speed.
- Blend on fool speed for about a minute, until the soup is creamy.
- Repeat with the rest of the soup, working in batches.

NUTRITION FACTS (PER SERVING)

Calories	361	
Total Fat	30.6g	39%
Saturated Fat	26.9g	134%
Cholesterol	0mg	0%
Sodium	78mg	3%
Total Carbohydrate	22.1g	8%
Dietary Fiber	5.5g	20%
Total Sugars	8.7g	
Protein	5.7g	

Meatballs with Ginger

| Prep time: 20 min | Cook time: 35 min | Servings: 4 |

Ingredients

- *1 lb. ground turkey*
- *1 small red onion, minced*
- *2 cloves garlic, minced*
- *1 tbsp minced fresh ginger*
- *1 tbsp lemon zest*
- *1 Serrano pepper, minced*
- *½ cup rice cauliflower*
- *tsp honey*
- *1 tsp salt*

Instructions

- Preheat a clean, lightly greased grill or drip pan.

- In a dish, combine the ground turkey with garlic, ginger, onions, lemon zest, Serrano, honey, and riced cauliflower and salt, and stir gently to distribute all the ingredients evenly.
- Roll the mixture into golf ball-sized balls, then carefully put 3 or 4 onto each skewer.
- Add the meatball skewers on a hot grill and grill, 4 to 5 minutes per side, until light charcoal develops on the outside and the meatballs are cooked through. When they're done, they should feel firm.
- Use the salad and rice to make small wraps with your choice of meatballs, pickles and sauces.

NUTRITION FACTS (PER SERVING)

Calories	251	
Total Fat	12.6g	16%
Saturated Fat	2.1g	11%
Cholesterol	116mg	39%
Sodium	708mg	31%
Total Carbohydrate	7.1g	3%
Dietary Fiber	1g	4%
Total Sugars	4.1g	
Protein	31.8g	

<u>*Tips: Korean cuisine usually likes to use large lettuce leaves for grilled meat, rice, kimchi, and sauces.*</u>

Mahi-Mahi Salad-Stuffed Avocado

| Prep time: 10 min | Cook time: 0 min | Servings: 2 |

Ingredients

- ⅔ *cup canned mahi-mahi*
- *2 tbsp basil pesto*
- *2 tbsp sour cream*
- *2 tbsp minced onion*
- *1 avocado*
- *2 cups baby kale*
- *10 thin wheat crackers*

Instructions

- Mix the mahi-mahi with the pesto, sour cream and onion.
- Serve over avocado and kale leaves with crackers on the side.

NUTRITION FACTS (PER SERVING)

Calories	300	
Total Fat	12.7g	29%
Saturated Fat	5.8g	29%
Cholesterol	28mg	9%
Sodium	168mg	7%
Total Carbohydrate	14.3g	5%
Dietary Fiber	7.9g	28%
Total Sugars	0.8g	
Protein	14.3g	

<u>*Tips: Avocados contain a monounsaturated fat called oleic acid. This amazing compound has been linked to decreased inflammation, according to research and studies.*</u>

Cod Salad with Eggs

| Prep time: 20 min | Cook time: 0 min | Servings: 4 |

Ingredients

- 2 large eggs
- 2 strips bacon
- ½ cup mayonnaise
- 2 tbsp Greek yogurt
- ⅛ tsp orange zest
- ½ stalk celery, thinly sliced
- 1 (5-ounce) cans cod
- 1 tbsp orange juice
- 1 green onion, sliced
- Kosher salt and freshly ground black pepper
- 1 small tomato, halved and cut into 8 slices
- A few whole leaves of lettuce

Instructions

- Put the eggs to a saucepan, add in approx. an inch of water.

- Bring to a boil, remove from heat, cover and let stand 8 minutes. Drain and immerse in ice water. When it is cold enough, peel and chop the eggs.
- While the eggs are cooking, cook the bacon in a large pan over medium heat for about 4 minutes per side, until golden brown and crisp. Place on a plate with paper towels. Crumble into bite-sized pieces.
- Whisk together the Greek yogurt, mayonnaise, orange zest and orange juice, celery, tuna oil, three-quarters of the chives, ¼ tsp of salt and several types of pepper flour in a bowl. Add the cod and three quarters of the bacon and egg and fold carefully (do not over mix). Season with salt and pepper if necessary.
- Sprinkle the tomatoes with ground pepper and salt. Stir in the lettuce leaves and garnish with a little cod salad. Add a slice of tomato. Sprinkle with the reserved chives, bacon and egg.

NUTRITION FACTS (PER SERVING)

Calories	332	
Total Fat	18.8g	24%
Saturated Fat	5.1g	26%
Cholesterol	141mg	47%
Sodium	535mg	23%
Total Carbohydrate	12.9g	5%
Dietary Fiber	0.5g	2%
Total Sugars	6.9g	
Protein	27.6g	

<u>Tips: Cod is a nutritious and tasty fish that is packed with lean protein, vitamins, and minerals. Cod may contain less omega-3 fatty acids than fatty fish, but it can still be part of a healthy diet.</u>

Chicken Chili

| Prep time: 15 min | Cook time: 30 min | Servings: 8 |

Ingredients

- *2 tbsp vegetable oil*
- *2 large onion, chopped*
- *1 red bell pepper, seeded and chopped*
- *1 green bell pepper, seeded and chopped*
- *1 stick of leek, chopped*
- *1 carrot, chopped*
- *4 garlic cloves (minced)*
- *1.5-pound lean ground chicken*
- *4 tbsp paprika*
- *4 tsp ground cumin*
- *1 tsp oregano*
- *1tsp ground coriander*
- *2 (14.5-ounce) can crushed tomatoes*

- 2(8-ounce) can unsalted tomato sauce
- 2 15-ounce cans pinto beans (drained)
- 8 tbsp fresh cream

Instructions

- Heat the vegetable oil in a saucepan. Add the onion, leek, red bell pepper, green bell pepper, carrot and garlic. Cook until onions are translucent (approx. 5 min).
- Disintegrate the grounded chicken in the pan and break it up with a wooden spoon. Cook until no longer pink inside, or about 5 minutes.
- Add the paprika, ground cumin, ground coriander and oregano.
- Add the tomatoes and tomato sauce and simmer for 10 min. Stir from time to time.
- Add the pinto beans, mix well and simmer for another 5 to 10 min.
- Serve in bowls. Add a tbsp fat-free fresh cream plus a little chopped fresh cilantro if you have it. Serve and enjoy!

NUTRITION FACTS (PER SERVING)		
Calories	602	
Total Fat	10.5g	13%
Saturated Fat	2.3g	12%
Cholesterol	47mg	16%
Sodium	632mg	27%
Total Carbohydrate	88.5g	32%
Dietary Fiber	23.6g	84%
Total Sugars	14.8g	
Protein	41.9g	

Tips: Add a can of drained sweet corn, which is a nice and tasty addition.

Kale and Cottage Pasta

| Prep time: 5 min | Cook time: 15 min | Servings: 4 |

Ingredients

- *1 ounce Gluten Free elbow macaroni or any type*
- *1 tsp coconut oil*
- *¼ cup onion, finely chopped*
- *1 garlic clove, minced*
- *5 cups fresh kale, roughly chopped*
- *½ ounce fresh parsley, chopped*
- *½ cup low-fat cottage cheese*
- *⅛ cup coconut milk*

Instructions

- Cook pasta according to package instructions.

- Melt the coconut oil in a saucepan, over medium heat. Add onion and garlic and sauté until onions are tender and fragrant (about 5 min). Be careful not to brown the garlic.
- Add the kale and parsley to the pan and stir until tender.
- Then add the cottage cheese and the coconut milk to the saucepan and stir well.
- Drain the pasta and keep about ¼ cup of the cooking water.
- Combine cooked pasta and cottage mixture in a large bowl. If it is too thick, add the cooking water to the mixture.
- Serve immediately with freshly ground black pepper.

NUTRITION FACTS (PER SERVING)

Calories	125	
Total Fat	3.7g	5%
Saturated Fat	3g	15%
Cholesterol	2mg	1%
Sodium	153mg	7%
Total Carbohydrate	16.4g	6%
Dietary Fiber	2.3g	8%
Total Sugars	0.8g	
Protein	7.7g	

Tips: If you add lemon to the cottage mixture gives this dish an extra shine.

Couscous Salad

| Prep time: 10 min | Cook time: 15 min | Servings: 4 |

Ingredients

- *½ cup uncooked Couscous*
- *1 cup fat-free, low-sodium vegetable broth*
- *½ cup fresh green peas*
- *½ cup chopped red pepper*
- *½ 15-oz. can Kidney beans*
- *½ cup grape tomatoes, halved*
- *⅛ cup finely chopped onion*
- *1 Serrano pepper, finely chopped*
- *⅛ cup chopped fresh basil*
- *Juice of 1 large lemon*

- 1-½ tbsp. olive oil
- ¼ tsp cumin

Instructions

- Rinse the Couscous well in a colander to remove the bitter layer.
- Place the Couscous in a 2-liter saucepan with the vegetable broth. Bring to a boil, cover and simmer for 10 to 15 minutes until the water is absorbed and the Couscous is tender. Let cool.
- Place the cooled cooked Couscous in a bowl with peas, red bell pepper, kidney beans, tomatoes, onions, Serrano and basil.
- In a small bowl, whisk together the lemon juice, olive oil and cumin.
- Drizzle and toss over the Couscous salad.

NUTRITION FACTS (PER SERVING)

Calories	164	
Total Fat	4g	5%
Saturated Fat	0.6g	3%
Cholesterol	0mg	0%
Sodium	200mg	9%
Total Carbohydrate	26.8g	10%
Dietary Fiber	4.2g	15%
Total Sugars	3.9g	
Protein	6g	

Tips: Whole grain couscous is a rich source of fiber. Fiber is good for you in many ways. It can keep your blood sugar from rising and keep you fuller for longer. It can also help lower cholesterol, which may lower your risk for heart disease.

Chicken Fajita Bowl

| Prep time: 10 min | Cook time: 10 min | Servings: 4 |

Ingredients

- *1 ½ tsp oregano*
- *1 tbsp chili powder*
- *½ tsp garlic, minced*
- *½ tsp onion powder*
- *1 tsp paprika*
- *1 ½ tsp salt*
- *¾ tsp black pepper*
- *1 ½ tsp cumin*
- *½ tsp basil*
- *1 ½ pounds chicken breasts cut into bit size pieces*
- *1 large onion diced*

- *1 red pepper diced*
- *1 yellow or orange pepper diced*
- *1 ½ tbsp coconut oil*

Instructions

- Combine oregano, chili powder, onion powder, garlic, paprika, salt, pepper, cumin and basil in a small bowl. Mix well.
- Add a tbsp of coconut oil in a saucepan and add the chicken and half of the spice mixer.
- Stir frequently until the meat is cooked through (about 5-7 min). Put in a bowl or plate.
- Add the rest of the oil, onion and peppers to the pan. Spread the rest of the spice mixer on top and cook, about 8 to 10 minutes, until tender.
- Serve the chicken, peppers and onions over romaine lettuce or cauliflower rice and garnish with avocado if desired.

NUTRITION FACTS (PER SERVING)

Calories	332	
Total Fat	9.3g	12%
Saturated Fat	4.5g	22%
Cholesterol	131mg	44%
Sodium	101mg	44%
Total Carbohydrate	9.8g	4%
Dietary Fiber	2.8g	10%
Total Sugars	4.5g	
Protein	50.9g	

Tips: Quick fajita marinade: in a large Ziploc bag, combine all the fajita marinade ingredients and the chicken breasts. Seal and let sit for a few minutes for the flavors to combine.

Quinoa Vegetable Soup with Beans

| Prep time: 10 min | Cook time: 60 min | Servings: 4 |

Ingredients

- *1 tsp garlic powder*
- *½ cup chopped onion*
- *1 medium carrot, peeled and chopped*
- *1 stalk leek, chopped*
- *cups vegetable broth*
- *½ cups fresh mushrooms, sliced*
- *½ cup pinto beans, rinsed*
- *¼ cup Quinoa*
- *½ tbsp tomato paste*
- *½ tsp dried basil*

- ½ tsp curry powder
- 1 bay leaf
- ½ tbsp cilantro finely chopped
- 1 tbsp fresh lime juice
- ½ tbsp Balsamic Vinegar
- ½ tsp salt
- ¼ tsp black pepper

Instructions

- Spray a 4-quart saucepan with a cooking spray.
- Add onion and garlic powder and sauté for 4 minutes, stirring occasionally.
- Add carrots and leek. Fry another 3 minutes, stirring occasionally.
- Combine 6 cups of vegetable broth along with the mushrooms, pinto beans, quinoa, tomato paste, basil, curry powder and bay leaf.
- Bring to a boil. Reduce the heat and simmer for 60 to 70 minutes, or until the pinto beans and quinoa are tender but not soft.
- Stir in the remaining broth, cilantro, lime juice, Balsamic Vinegar, salt and pepper.

NUTRITION FACTS (PER SERVING)		
Calories	200	
Total Fat	2.5g	3%
Saturated Fat	0.5g	3%
Cholesterol	0mg	0%
Sodium	1080mg	47%
Total Carbohydrate	31.8g	12%
Dietary Fiber	6.1g	22%
Total Sugars	4.6g	
Protein	12.9g	

Red Lentil and Chickpeas Soup

| Prep time: 20 min | Cook time: 30 min | Servings: 4 |

Ingredients

- *1 tsp coconut oil*
- *1 cup finely chopped onion*
- *1 small leek stalk, diced*
- *1 tsp garlic powder*
- *½ tbsp ground cumin*
- *½ tbsp paprika*
- *½ cup rinsed red lentils*
- *1 (15-ounce) cans reduced-sodium chickpeas, drained and rinsed*
- *½ (14.5-ounce) can diced tomatoes*
- *1 cup fat-free, low-sodium vegetable broth*
- *1 cup water*

Instructions

- Heat the coconut oil in a saucepan, over medium heat.
- Fry the onions, leek and garlic powder for about 4 to 5 minutes, until just tender.
- Sprinkle with cumin and paprika and cook 1 minute until fragrant.
- Add the red lentils, chickpeas, tomatoes, water and broth.
- Bring to a boil and cover. Simmer for around 25 minutes or until lentils are tender.
- Serve and enjoy!

NUTRITION FACTS (PER SERVING)		
Calories	234	
Total Fat	2.6g	3%
Saturated Fat	1.1g	5%
Cholesterol	0mg	0%
Sodium	341mg	15%
Total Carbohydrate	41g	15%
Dietary Fiber	9.1g	32%
Total Sugars	8.5g	
Protein	12.7g	

Tips: Lentils absorb a lot of flavor when cooked. Use broth or broth in place of water and add flavors such as garlic, herbs and spices to the liquid while the lentils are cooking.

Carrot and Zucchini Soup

| Prep time: 20 min | Cook time: 30 min | Servings: 4 |

Ingredients

- *1 tsp coconut oil*
- *1 small onion, finely chopped*
- *½ lb. carrots, peeled and sliced*
- *½ lb. zucchini, unpeeled and sliced*
- *½ cup pumpkin chopped*
- *½ cup sweet potato diced*
- *1 tsp curry powder*
- *2 cups low-sodium vegetable broth,*
- *⅛ cup fresh basil*

Instructions

- Sauté onions in a pot for 5 minutes or until just tender.

- Add the carrots and zucchini sweet potato and pumpkin, then the curry powder.
- Stir for 1 to 2 minutes. Add the vegetable broth and bring to a boil.
- Reduce the heat and simmer for 20 minutes. At the end, add the chopped basil.
- Transfer the soup to a blender and mix gently, working in two batches.
- Serve and enjoy!

NUTRITION FACTS (PER SERVING)

Calories	100	
Total Fat	2.1g	3%
Saturated Fat	1.2g	6%
Cholesterol	0mg	0%
Sodium	438mg	19%
Total Carbohydrate	16.7g	6%
Dietary Fiber	3.6g	13%
Total Sugars	6.9g	
Protein	4.6g	

<u>*Tips: Steam expands quickly in a blender and can cause ingredients to splash all over or burn. To avoid this, fill the blender only a third of the way up, lift the lid and cover with a kitchen towel or aluminum foil while blending.*</u>

Hemp Broiled Tilapia with Ginger

| Prep time: 4 h | Cook time: 10 min | Servings: 8 |

Ingredients

- 8 (6 ounces each) Tilapia fillets
- 1 cup coconut aminos
- 1 cup apple cider vinegar
- tbsp coconut oil
- tbsp fresh ginger, peeled and minced
- tsp garlic powder
- 1 cup leek finely chopped
- ½ cup Hemp Seeds

Instructions

- In a large glass bowl, combine the coconut aminos, apple cider vinegar, coconut oil, garlic powder, ginger and half the chopped leek.

- Place the Tilapia in a large zippered bag, pour the marinade liquid into the bag, wring out any excess air, and seal it.
- Marinate the Tilapia in the refrigerator for 2 to 4 hours.
- Preheat the grill for 5 minutes. Remove the fillets from the bag and place them skin side down on a baking sheet covered with a silicone baking mat. Sprinkle liberally with hemp seeds and pat firmly against the Tilapia. Tilapia should be completely covered with hemp seeds.
- Place the pan on the top rack of your oven (or under the grill if you have a separate grill) and cook for 7-8 minutes, or until the fillets are flaky but still sag slightly when pressed
- While the fillets are cooking, pour the remaining marinade into a saucepan and bring to a boil. Then, simmer and reduce while the fillets are cooking.
- Serve the Tilapia with the reduced marinade and garnish with the remaining leeks or herbs of your choice.

NUTRITION FACTS (PER SERVING)

Calories	250	
Total Fat	11.5g	15%
Saturated Fat	6.6g	33%
Cholesterol	55mg	18%
Sodium	79mg	3%
Total Carbohydrate	11g	4%
Dietary Fiber	0.9g	3%
Total Sugars	0.9g	
Protein	24.1g	

<u>*Tips: Avoid using glass cookware when cooking or if a recipe calls for adding liquid to a hot pot as the glass may explode. Even though this indicates that they are oven or heat resistant, tempered glass products can - and sometimes do.*</u>

Baked Chicken with Barley

| Prep time: 10 min | Cook time: 10 min | Servings: 8 |

Ingredients

- 8 boneless, skinless chicken breasts (5 to 6 ounce each)
- 2cups barley (uncooked)
- 4 cups fat-free, low-sodium chicken broth
- 2 (14ounce) can dice tomatoes (undrained)
- 1 medium onion, chopped
- 1 cup carrot, sliced
- ½ cup green peas
- 1 tsp garlic powder
- 1 tsp dried basil
- 6 cups fresh baby kale, chopped

Instructions

- Preheat the oven to 400 F.
- Put the chicken breasts in a single layer in a baking dish that can accommodate the chicken in a single layer.
- Combine uncooked barley, chicken broth, tomatoes, onions, carrot, green peas, garlic powder and basil in a medium bowl.
- Add the chopped kale.
- Pour the mixture over the chicken.
- Cover with foil and bake, 35 to 40 minutes, until the chicken is cooked through and the barley is tender.
- Serve and enjoy!

NUTRITION FACTS (PER SERVING)

Calories	497	
Total Fat	11.5g	15%
Saturated Fat	3.1g	15%
Cholesterol	125mg	42%
Sodium	546mg	24%
Total Carbohydrate	48.5g	18%
Dietary Fiber	11.6g	41%
Total Sugars	5.7g	
Protein	49.9g	

Tips: The secret to juicy baked chicken breasts is cooking them at the right temperature, and 190 ° C is the best temperature for baked chicken breasts.

Fresh Kale Garlic Soup

| Prep time: 10 min | Cook time: 25 min | Servings: 8 |

Ingredients

- *4 tsp coconut oil*
- *2 medium Sweet potato, peeled and cubed*
- *1 medium onion, finely chopped*
- *2 stalk leeks, finely chopped*
- *2 tsp. garlic powder*
- *2 cups vegetable broth*
- *2 cups water*
- *2 cups coconut milk*
- *2 (6-ounce) bag baby kale, divided*
- *Freshly ground black pepper, to taste*
- *Kosher salt, to taste*

Instructions

- In a large saucepan or Dutch oven, heat the coconut oil.
- Sauté the sweet potato, onion, leek and garlic powder for 5 minutes.
- Add the vegetable broth, water and coconut milk. Bring to a boil and cover, then simmer for 10 minutes.
- Add kale, cover and simmer for another 10 minutes.
- Let it slightly cool, then transfer to a blender. Work in two batches if necessary, to prevent hot soup from spilling into the blender during blending.
- Season to taste and serve.

NUTRITION FACTS (PER SERVING)

Calories	235	
Total Fat	17.1g	22%
Saturated Fat	14.8g	74%
Cholesterol	0mg	0%
Sodium	255mg	11%
Total Carbohydrate	18.8g	7%
Dietary Fiber	3.7g	13%
Total Sugars	5.6g	
Protein	5g	

Tips: kale soup will keep for a few days in an airtight container in the fridge.

Glazed Tempeh

| Prep time: 5 min | Cook time: 15 min | Servings: 8 |

Ingredients

- *2 pounds tempeh, trimmed*
- *2 tbsp. coconut oil*
- *½ cup apple cider vinegar*
- *4 tbsp. maple syrup*
- *2 tbsp. Dijon mustard*

Instructions

- Cut the tempeh into 1-inch slices. Heat the coconut oil in a large skillet over medium heat.
- In the meantime, preheat the oven to 375 F and spray a baking sheet with non-stick cooking spray.

- Fry the tempeh for a minute on each side and place them on a baking sheet.
- Whisk the vinegar, maple syrup and Dijon mustard in a small bowl. Generously brush the tempeh with glaze.
- Bake for 10 minutes.

NUTRITION FACTS (PER SERVING)

Calories	280	
Total Fat	15.8g	20%
Saturated Fat	5.5g	27%
Cholesterol	0mg	0%
Sodium	56mg	2%
Total Carbohydrate	17.7g	6%
Dietary Fiber	0.1g	0%
Total Sugars	6g	
Protein	21.2g	

Tips: Tempeh is very nutritious. Among others, it is a rich source of protein, iron, phosphorus and calcium and it is low in carbohydrates and sodium.

Vegetable Stew

| Prep time: 10 min | Cook time: 7 h | Servings: 12 |

Ingredients

- *3 tsp garlic powder*
- *2 medium onion, chopped*
- *4 leek stalks, chopped*
- *4 large carrots, sliced thick*
- *2 small Acorn squash, peeled, seeded, and cut into 1 ½-inch chunks*
- *1 (8-ounce) package sliced mushrooms*
- *1 cup zucchini*
- *1-pound small sweet potatoes*
- *2 (15-ounce) can low sodium navy beans rinsed and drained*
- *3 cup vegetable broth*
- *2 (15-ounce) can tomatoes*
- *2 bay leaf*

Instructions

- Place the garlic powder, onion and all the vegetables in a 4–5-quart slow cooker.
- Add the navy beans, vegetable broth, tomatoes and bay leaf.
- Simmer for 5 to 7 hours until the vegetables are tender.
- Serve with crusty bread and enjoy!

NUTRITION FACTS (PER SERVING)		
Calories	128	
Total Fat	1.2g	1%
Saturated Fat	0.1g	1%
Cholesterol	0mg	0%
Sodium	374mg	16%
Total Carbohydrate	24.6g	9%
Dietary Fiber	6.4g	23%
Total Sugars	5.2g	
Protein	7.2g	

Tips: This slow cooker vegetable stew is even better the next day, and when refrigerated and covered, it will last up to 5 days.

Turkey and Orzo Soup

| Prep time: 15 min | Cook time: 2h | Servings: 5 |

Ingredients

- 2-½ cups chicken broth
- 1 skinless, boneless turkey breast halves
- ½ cup diced leek
- ½ cup diced onion
- ⅛ cup diced carrots
- ⅛ cup green peas
- ¼ cup zucchini
- ¼ cup cauliflower
- ⅛ cup corn
- ⅛ cup drained and rinsed Kidney beans
- ½ tsp dried Rosemary

- ½ tsp ground black pepper
- ½ tsp salt
- 1 bay leaf
- ¾ cup orzo

Instructions

- Bring the chicken broth to a boil in a pot. Cook the turkey breasts in boiling water until no longer pink in the center (about 20 minutes). Using a slotted spoon, remove the turkey from the chicken broth and chop it with a fork.
- Stir the grated turkey, leek, onion, carrots, green peas, corn, cauliflower, zucchini, kidney beans, rosemary, pepper, salt and bay leaves in the chicken broth and cook until vegetables are cooked through - slightly tender and the flavors of the soup have combined (about 20 minutes).
- Add the orzo to the soup and simmer for about 30 min until the orzo is tender.

NUTRITION FACTS (PER SERVING)		
Calories	173	
Total Fat	2.3g	3%
Saturated Fat	0.6g	3%
Cholesterol	13mg	4%
Sodium	557mg	24%
Total Carbohydrate	27.7g	10%
Dietary Fiber	2.6g	9%
Total Sugars	1.9g	
Protein	10.3g	

Tips: Whole-wheat orzo is a rich source of fiber, which can help improve digestion.

DESSERT RECIPES

Nutmeg Apple Frozen Yogurt

| Prep time: 5 min | Cook time: 40 min | Servings: 4 |

Ingredients

- *2 apples halves*
- *1 cup Greek yogurt*
- *½ cup coconut sugar*
- *¼ tsp ground nutmeg*
- *⅛ tsp ground cinnamon*

Instructions

- Puree the apple in a blender.

- Combine apple, Greek yogurt, coconut sugar, cinnamon and nutmeg in an ice cream jar.
- Freeze for two or more hours.

NUTRITION FACTS (PER SERVING)

Calories	91	
Total Fat	1.1g	1%
Saturated Fat	0.8g	4%
Cholesterol	3mg	1%
Sodium	21mg	1%
Total Carbohydrate	15.5g	6%
Dietary Fiber	2.6g	9%
Total Sugars	10.6g	
Protein	5.2g	

Tips: Apples are packed with carbohydrates that give you instant energy.

Chocolate Cookies without Flour

| Prep time: 5 min | Cook time: 15 min | Servings: 8 |

Ingredients

- ½ cup powdered sugar
- 1 tsp corn-starch
- ⅛ cup unsweetened cocoa powder
- ¹⁄₁₆ tsp salt
- 1 large egg whites
- ½ tsp vanilla extract
- ¼ cup chocolate chips

Instructions

- Preheat the oven to 350 degrees F. Line 2 large baking sheets with parchment paper. Coat the paper with cooking spray.

- Combine powdered sugar, corn-starch cocoa powder and salt in a medium bowl.
- Beat the egg whites in a bowl, using a fork or an electric mixer, until a bit firm.
- Using a rubber spatula, stir in the vanilla and cocoa powder mixture until just combined. Stir in the chocolate chips (or pieces).
- Use the spoons to drop the dough into the prepared baking sheets, leaving about 2 inches of space between each cookie. Bake one baking sheet at a time until cookies start to crack on top, 12 to 14 minutes.
- Let cool slightly in the pan before placing it on a wire rack to cool completely.

NUTRITION FACTS (PER SERVING)		
Calories	67	
Total Fat	1.8g	2%
Saturated Fat	1.2g	6%
Cholesterol	1mg	0%
Sodium	28mg	1%
Total Carbohydrate	12.3g	4%
Dietary Fiber	0.6g	2%
Total Sugars	10.1g	
Protein	1.1g	

Chocolate Biscotti with Walnuts

| Prep time: 5 min | Cook time: 15 min | Servings: 12 |

Ingredients

- *1 -¼ cups whole wheat flour*
- *1 cup coconut sugar*
- *3/2 cup unsweetened cocoa powder*
- *eggs*
- *½ tsp vanilla extract*
- *½ tsp baking soda*
- *¼ tsp salt*
- *½ cup walnuts*

Instructions

- Preheat the oven to 180 ° C.
- Mix all the ingredients except the walnuts in a bowl. Mix well with a spoon.
- Add walnuts until well combined.
- The dough should be a bit thick and sticky.

- Place the first half of the dough on a 10 x 15-inch baking sheet coated with nonstick spray. Form a slightly rounded 4-by-12-inch rod about ¾ of an inch thick.
- Repeat with the second half of the dough. Put it on a second baking sheet and bake for 30 min.
- Take the sheets out of the oven and reduce the temperature to 170 ° C. Let the cookies cool for 20 to 25 min, then cut them into ½-inch-thick slices.
- Place the cut slices face down on the baking sheet and bake for another 15 min.
- Flip the cookies to the other side and bake for another 15 min or until very crisp.

NUTRITION FACTS (PER SERVING)		
Calories	85	
Total Fat	5.3g	7%
Saturated Fat	1.3g	6%
Cholesterol	27mg	9%
Sodium	118mg	5%
Total Carbohydrate	9.9g	4%
Dietary Fiber	4.3g	15%
Total Sugars	0.4g	
Protein	4.7g	

Tips: Store in an airtight container. It will keep for several weeks.

Chilled Banana Pudding

| Prep time: 20 min | Cook time: 20 min | Servings: 4 |

Ingredients

- ½ *cup coconut sugar*
- ¼ *cup corn-starch*
- *1 egg, beaten*
- ½ *(12 fluid ounce) can heavy cream*
- ¾ *cups coconut milk*
- *1 tsp vanilla extract*
- ½ *(12 ounces) package vanilla wafers or your choice*
- *2 bananas, sliced*

Instructions

- In a saucepan over medium heat, combine the coconut sugar, potato starch, egg, heavy cream and coconut milk. Mix well and stir until thickened. Remove the stove, add the vanilla and mix well.
- Put a layer of cookies in a large bowl or saucepan. Pour the pudding over the cookies.
- Garnish it with a layer of banana slices. Place in the refrigerator until it cools.

NUTRITION FACTS (PER SERVING)

Calories	261	
Total Fat	14.2g	18%
Saturated Fat	10.7g	54%
Cholesterol	49mg	16%
Sodium	60mg	3%
Total Carbohydrate	31.6g	11%
Dietary Fiber	2.8g	10%
Total Sugars	12.7g	
Protein	3.7g	

Tips: To thicken the instant pudding with corn-starch, make porridge by mixing equal parts corn-starch and water, heat the instant pudding, then add the corn-starch mixture. The reason for making a paste instead of adding powdered corn starch directly to the pudding is to prevent lumps from forming.

Oatmeal Cookies with Nutmeg- Apricots

| Prep time: 5 min | Cook time: 15 min | Servings: 12 |

Ingredients

- ½ cup all-purpose flour
- ½ tsp baking powder
- ½ tsp ground nutmeg
- ¼ tsp salt
- ½ cup coconut sugar
- 3 tbsp coconut oil
- 1 large egg
- 1 tsp vanilla extract
- ½ cup old-fashioned rolled oats
- ¼ cup apricots

Instructions

- Preheat the oven to 350° F.

- Lightly coat a baking sheet with cooking spray.
- In a medium bowl, whisk together all-purpose flour, baking powder, nutmeg and salt.
- Whisk together the coconut sugar, coconut oil, egg and vanilla in a bowl.
- Add the flour mixture, oats and apricots and stir with a wooden spoon until combined.
- Place flat balls of dough on the prepared baking sheet and bake 12 cookies per set.
- Bake, 12 to 14 minutes, until the bottom is golden. Let the baking sheet cool for 5 minutes before placing it on a wire rack to cool completely. Repeat with the rest of the dough.

NUTRITION FACTS (PER SERVING)		
Calories	83	
Total Fat	3.8g	5%
Saturated Fat	2.1g	10%
Cholesterol	23mg	8%
Sodium	79mg	3%
Total Carbohydrate	9.6g	4%
Dietary Fiber	0.9g	3%
Total Sugars	0.4g	
Protein	2.3g	

Almond Butter- Quinoa Energy Balls

| Prep time: 5 min | Cook time: 15 min | Servings: 24 |

Ingredients

- ¾ cup honey
- 1 cup quinoa
- ½ cup natural almond butter
- Flax seeds for garnish

Instructions

- Combine the honey, quinoa and almond butter in a food processor and process until very finely chopped.
- Roll into 24 balls (a scant tbsp each).
- Garnish with flax seeds, if desired.

NUTRITION FACTS (PER SERVING)

Calories	60	
Total Fat	0.6g	1%
Saturated Fat	0.1g	0%
Cholesterol	0mg	0%
Sodium	1mg	0%
Total Carbohydrate	13.3g	5%
Dietary Fiber	0.6g	2%
Total Sugars	8.7g	
Protein	1.1g	

Tips: Refrigerate for at least 15 minutes and up to 1 week.

Almond Barley Pudding

| Prep time: 10 min | Cook time: 25 min | Servings: 8 |

Ingredients

- 2 cups almond milk
- 1 cup barley
- ½ cup raisins
- ½ cup honey
- 2-3 tsp freshly grated lemon zest
- 1 tsp vanilla extract
- Pinch salt
- Ground cinnamon for dusting (optional)

Instructions

- Combine almond milk, barley, raisins and honey in a medium heavy saucepan. Bring to a boil while stirring.

- Lower the heat and simmer, uncovered, while stirring frequently, until the barley is tender and the pudding is creamy (20 to 25 minutes). Stir almost constantly towards the end to avoid burns.
- Add the lemon zest, vanilla and salt and pour the pudding into a bowl or individual bowls. Let cool slightly.
- Eat immediately or eat when cooled.
- Sprinkle with some cinnamon if desired.

NUTRITION FACTS (PER SERVING)

Calories	383	
Total Fat	22g	28%
Saturated Fat	19.2g	96%
Cholesterol	0mg	0%
Sodium	38mg	2%
Total Carbohydrate	46.9g	17%
Dietary Fiber	6.5g	23%
Total Sugars	26.1g	
Protein	5.3g	

Tips: If your barley pudding seems a bit too thin, you can easily thicken it with a slurry. Use a single tsp corn-starch with a tbsp of water.

Pecans-Cinnamon Pumpkin Custards

| Prep time: 10 min | Cook time: 20 min | Servings: 4 |

Ingredients

- ½ cup coconut milk
- ½ cup canned pumpkin
- 1 egg, lightly beaten
- ½ cup honey
- ¼ cup refrigerated or frozen egg product (thawed before use)
- 1 tsp vanilla
- ½ tsp ground cinnamon
- ⅛ tsp salt
- ⅛ tsp ground allspice
- ⅛ cup chopped pecans
- ⅛ cup quinoa
- ½ tbsp butter, melted

Instructions

- Preheat the oven to 350 degrees F. Brush eight 6-ounce ramekins with cooking spray. Place the ramekins in two 2-liter square saucepans.
- In a medium bowl, combine coconut milk, pumpkin, eggs, honey, egg products and vanilla. Sift ½ tsp ground cinnamon, salt and allspice into a small bowl. Add seasoning mix to pumpkin mixture; Beat with a whisk until everything is combined.
- In the small bowl with the spice blend, combine the nuts, quinoa, brown sugar and the remaining ¼ tsp ground cinnamon. Add the melted butter; Stir until everything is well combined.
- Distribute the pumpkin mixture evenly over prepared dishes. Place the cooking utensils on the rack so that there is enough boiling water in the baking tins up to the middle of the sides of the tins. Bake for 15 minutes.
- Carefully pour about 1 tbsp of the nut mixture over each. Bake for another 15 to 20 minutes or until a knife comes out clean near the center.
- Take out shapes from the water; Let cool on the rack for 30 minutes. Cover and refrigerate for up to 4 hours before serving.
- To serve, top with whipped dessert and, if desired, sprinkle with freshly grated nutmeg.

NUTRITION FACTS (PER SERVING)

Calories	271	
Total Fat	10.4g	13%
Saturated Fat	7.7g	39%
Cholesterol	45mg	15%
Sodium	139mg	6%
Total Carbohydrate	43.3g	16%
Dietary Fiber	2.2g	8%
Total Sugars	37.1g	
Protein	4.9g	

Tips: You will use 1 whole egg as a substitute for the frozen egg product.

Coconut Mug Brownie

| Prep time: 5 min | Cook time: 10 min | Servings: 2 |

Ingredients

- *2 tbsp butter*
- *4 tbsp unsweetened coconut milk*
- *½ tsp vanilla extract*
- *3 tbsp coconut flour*
- *2 tbsp maple syrup*
- *2 tbsp unsweetened cocoa powder*
- *¼ tsp salt*

- *4 tsp mini chocolate chips (Optional)*

Instructions

- Pour the butter into a small microwave-safe 2 coffee cup and place it in the microwave for 15-20 seconds until melted.
- Let cool for 1 minute. Stir in the coconut milk and vanilla. Add the flour, maple syrup, cocoa and salt in both cups; keep beating until everything is completely incorporated.
- If using, add in the chocolate chips.
- Microwave until firm to the touch and not shiny, 30 to 40 seconds. Let stand 8 to 10 minutes.

NUTRITION FACTS (PER SERVING)

Calories	378	
Total Fat	24.7g	32%
Saturated Fat	18.3g	92%
Cholesterol	31mg	10%
Sodium	468mg	20%
Total Carbohydrate	37.2g	14%
Dietary Fiber	10g	36%
Total Sugars	18.1g	
Protein	5.4g	

Tips: Once the brownies are cooked and slightly cooled, add your favorite frosting.

No-Bake Cookies

| Prep time: 10 min | Cook time: 0 min | Servings: 8 |

Ingredients

- 16 Pretzels, finely ground
- ½ cup apricots
- ½ cup smooth natural almond butter
- 2 tbsp plus 2 tsp maple syrup
- 4 tsp unsweetened coconut (ground)

Instructions

- Combine ground Pretzels, apricot, almond butter and maple syrup in a small bowl.

- Shape 15 or 16 cookies.
- Roll them in the coconut crumbs until evenly coated.

NUTRITION FACTS (PER SERVING)

Calories	337	
Total Fat	9.9g	13%
Saturated Fat	1.1g	5%
Cholesterol	0mg	0%
Sodium	815mg	35%
Total Carbohydrate	55.1g	20%
Dietary Fiber	4.1g	14%
Total Sugars	6.1g	
Protein	9.9g	

Tips: If the dough seems too soft, chill it for 10 to 15 minutes before portioning.

Mini Fruit Pizzas With Pears

| Prep time: 10 min | Cook time: 0 min | Servings: 4 |

Ingredients

- *1 pear, sliced crosswise into 4 slices (¼ inch thick), seeds removed*
- *4 tbsp peanut butter*
- *4 tbsp mini chocolate chips*
- *2 tsp chopped salted roasted almonds*
- *2 tsp maple syrup*
- *A few graham crackers*

Instructions

- Brush each pears slice with 1 tbsp of peanut butter.
- Lay on top of the cracker.

- Garnish with 1 tbsp of chocolate chips, ½ tsp of almonds and ½ tsp of maple syrup.

NUTRITION FACTS (PER SERVING)

Calories	154	
Total Fat	9.7g	12%
Saturated Fat	2.4g	12%
Cholesterol	0mg	0%
Sodium	95mg	4%
Total Carbohydrate	14.4g	5%
Dietary Fiber	2.2g	8%
Total Sugars	8.7g	
Protein	4.6g	

Tips: pears are rich in pectin, a fiber that nourishes gut bacteria. You can use other fruit or nuts for the mini pizzas, such as blueberries, strawberries or bananas.

Blueberry Oats Bars

| Prep time: 10 min | Cook time: 0 min | Servings: 8 |

Ingredients

- ½ cup almond flour
- 6 tbsp. coconut oil
- ¼ cup plus 1 tablespoon, coconut sugar, divided
- ⅛ cup toasted walnuts, roughly chopped
- ½ cup old-fashioned rolled oats, divided
- ¼ tsp baking soda
- ¼ tsp kosher salt
- 1 (6-ounce) container of fresh blueberries

Instructions

- Preheat the oven to 375 ° F.

- Line an 8-inch pan with baking paper, leaving a 1-inch overhang on two sides.
- Combine almond flour, coconut oil and ¼ cup coconut sugar in a food processor 10 to 12 times until it forms a coarse texture. Transfer ⅓ cup to a bowl and add the walnuts and ¼ cup of the oatmeal. Squeeze to form small lumps; fresh.
- In the food processor, add the baking soda, salt and the remaining cup of oats to the mixture. Pulse until just incorporated, 12 to 15 times. Press into the bottom of the pan. Bake for 14 to 16 minutes until golden brown.
- Crush 1 container of blueberries and the remaining tbsp of coconut sugar in a bowl. Spread over the pre-cooked crust. Spread the remaining blueberries from the bowl and the cooled breadcrumb mixture on top.
- Bake for 40 to 45 minutes or until golden on top. Let cool in the saucepan for 30 minutes then transfer the overhang to the wire rack to cool completely.

NUTRITION FACTS (PER SERVING)

Calories	165	
Total Fat 15.1g		19%
Saturated Fat 9.2g		46%
Cholesterol 0mg		0%
Sodium 114mg		5%
Total Carbohydrate 7.1g		3%
Dietary Fiber 1.6g		6%
Total Sugars 2.4g		
Protein 2.5g		

<u>Tips: According to some studies, a bowl of blueberries can boost immunity and reduce the risk of diabetes, obesity and heart disease.</u>

Green Tea Maple syrup Frozen Yogurt

| Prep time: 10 min | Cook time: 0 min | Servings: 4 |

Ingredients

- *1-½ cup Greek yogurt*
- *1 cup half-and-half*
- *½ cup coconut sugar*
- *¼ cup maple syrup*
- *1-½ tbsp matcha green tea powder*
- *1 tsp. vanilla extract*
- *⅛ tsp salt*

Instructions

- Whip the yogurt half and half with coconut sugar, maple syrup, matcha, vanilla and salt.

- Leave to rest for 5 minutes.
- Beat until the coconut sugar has dissolved. Refrigerate for a few hours or until very cold.
- Pour the mixture into a bowl of an electric refrigerator and process it according to the manufacturer's instructions.
- Freeze 1 hour before serving.

NUTRITION FACTS (PER SERVING)		
Calories	183	
Total Fat	8g	10%
Saturated Fat	5.1g	25%
Cholesterol	25mg	8%
Sodium	122mg	5%
Total Carbohydrate	20.3g	7%
Dietary Fiber	0.3g	1%
Total Sugars	14g	
Protein	7.2g	

Tips: Store for up to 1 week.

Raspberry Cobbler

| Prep time: 10 min | Cook time: 45 min | Servings: 2 |

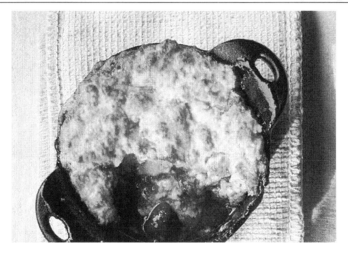

Ingredients

- ⅛ cup coconut oil
- ½ cup all-purpose flour
- 1 tsp. baking powder
- ¼ tsp. fine salt
- ½ cup coconut milk
- ⅙ cup maple syrup
- ½ tsp pure vanilla extract
- 2 cups fresh raspberries

Instructions

- Preheat the oven to 350 degrees F.

- Place coconut oil in 10 ½ inch cast iron pan or heavy-duty 9 x 13" baking dish and place in the oven for 5-7 minutes to heat.
- Meanwhile, combine the all-purpose flour, baking powder and salt in a bowl. Add the coconut milk, maple syrup and vanilla and stir to combine.
- Take the hot pan out of the oven. Combine the flour and the oil mixtures together. Return the batter to the hot pan and pour the raspberries over it. Bake for 30 to 35 minutes, until the pastry is golden brown and the pastry has risen.
- Place on a wire rack to chill.

NUTRITION FACTS (PER SERVING)		
Calories	312	
Total Fat	11.4g	27%
Saturated Fat	18.2g	91%
Cholesterol	0mg	0%
Sodium	155mg	7%
Total Carbohydrate	30.4g	11%
Dietary Fiber	5.1g	18%
Total Sugars	11.6g	
Protein	3g	

<u>*Tips: Serve Raspberry Cobbler with ice cream*</u>

Blueberry Ice Cream

| Prep time: 10 min | Cook time: 45 min | Servings: 4 |

Ingredients

- ½ lb. frozen blueberries
- ½ cup Sour Cream
- ⅛ cup honey
- ¼ tsp. vanilla extract
- Blueberries for garnish

Instructions

- Finely chop ¼ frozen blueberries with the blade of a knife. Transfer the berries to a metal bowl.
In a food processor, chop the remaining ¾ of frozen blueberries, add sour cream, honey and vanilla and mix until smooth.

- Transfer in a bowl with the chopped blueberries. Stir until everything is well combined.
- Cover and freeze for about 1 hour. It should be firm, but not to hard. Garnish with fresh blueberries.

NUTRITION FACTS (PER SERVING)

Calories	127	
Total Fat	6.2g	8%
Saturated Fat	3.8g	19%
Cholesterol	13mg	4%
Sodium	16mg	1%
Total Carbohydrate	18.2g	7%
Dietary Fiber	1.4g	5%
Total Sugars	14.4g	
Protein	1.4g	

Tips: If the ice is not beaten fast enough, larger ice crystals can form, which will make the ice too hard when it freezes. The faster the agitation, the more air is incorporated, which prevents it from freezing so badly.

Baked Pears with Quinoa

| Prep time: 20 min | Cook time: 45 min | Servings: 4 |

Ingredients

- *4 pears, bottoms sliced so pears stand*
- *½ fresh lime, halved*
- *tbsp unsalted butter*
- *tbsp coconut sugar*
- *$\frac{1}{16}$ tsp ground cinnamon*
- *Pinch ground black pepper*
- *½ cup rice wine*
- *½ cup coconut milk, heated*
- *1 tsp finely grated lime zest*
- *1 cup cooked quinoa*
- *Low-fat plain yogurt*

Instructions

- Preheat the oven to 375 ° F. Slice the top third of each pear. Using a spoon, hollow out the pear meat, 2 inches in diameter.
- Rub the cut part with lime and place the pears in a 9-inch square baking dish. Cut the carved parts of the pears without seeds and save them.
- Melt the coconut oil in a small saucepan then add 2 tbsp of coconut sugar, cinnamon and pepper and cook until smooth.
- Brush the inside of the pears with the oil mixture. Pour the rice wine into the bottom of the baking dish. Cover the plate with foil and bake for about 30 min, until the pears are tender.
- Remove the foil and cook for further 5 min. Transfer the pears to a dish. Carefully filter the cooking liquid into a small saucepan and bring to a boil.
- Cook 5 min until everything is reduced and thickened.
- While the pears cook, combine the hot milk, the remaining coconut sugar, the reserved chopped pears and the lime zest in the hot quinoa and cook for a few minutes.
- Spread the quinoa over the baked pears.
- Top each pear with a tbsp of yogurt and drizzle with reduced rice wine.

NUTRITION FACTS (PER SERVING)

Calories	521	
Total Fat	15.8g	20%
Saturated Fat	10.3g	51%
Cholesterol	15mg	5%
Sodium	340mg	15%
Total Carbohydrate	90g	33%
Dietary Fiber	10.4g	37%
Total Sugars	29.5g	
Protein	8.3g	

Tips: Quinoa and brown rice contain similar amounts of calories and micronutrients per cup, and similar amounts of fiber. However, quinoa has a bit more protein and less carbohydrate per serving, which makes it much more beneficial for your diet.

Quinoa Cookies

| Prep time: 10 min | Cook time: 30 min | Servings: 8 |

Ingredients

- ¼ cup almond flour
- ⅛ cup coconut flour
- ¼ cup coconut sugar
- ¼ tsp ground cinnamon
- 1 pinch Kosher salt
- ½ cup quinoa
- ½ cup unsweetened shredded coconut
- ¼ cup almond
- ⅛ cup apricots
- ⅛ cup dried blueberries
- ⅛ cup pumpkin seeds
- ¼ cup coconut oil
- 1-½ tbsp maple syrup
- ¼ tsp baking soda

- 1-½ tbsp boiling water

Instructions

- Preheat the oven to 350° F.
- Lay parchment paper into two baking sheets.
- Combine the flour, coconut sugar, cinnamon and salt in a large bowl. Add the quinoa and coconut and stir. Add the nuts, apricots, blueberries and pumpkin seeds.
- Melt the coconut oil and maple syrup in a pan. In a small bowl, combine the baking powder and boiling water, then add it to the butter mixture.
- Make a well in the center of the quinoa mixture, pour in the butter mixture and mix it.
- Shape the mixture into 8 balls (about ¼ cup each) with wet hands and place them on the prepared leaves spaced 1 ½ inches apart. Gently squeeze each ball to a thickness of 1 cm and cook until golden brown, 16 to 17 minutes. Let cool completely on baking sheets.

NUTRITION FACTS (PER SERVING)

Calories	234	
Total Fat	18g	23%
Saturated Fat	11.4g	57%
Cholesterol	0mg	0%
Sodium	73mg	3%
Total Carbohydrate	14.8g	5%
Dietary Fiber	3.2g	11%
Total Sugars	2.9g	
Protein	4.6g	

Tips: Mix all the dough in advance and store it in the fridge for 3-4 days or more in the freezer. I like to shape shortbread cookie dough into rods for cutting and baking, or molding batches of chocolate cookie dough to shape with a spoon.

Delicious Nutmeg Baked Peaches

| Prep time: 15 min | Cook time: 45 min | Servings: 4 |

Ingredients

- ½ tsp coconut oil
- 1 tbsp coconut sugar
- 1-½ tsp vanilla sugar
- 1-½ tsp ground nutmeg
- 4 large peaches - peeled, cored, and sliced
- 1 ½ tbsp water

Instructions

- Preheat the oven to 175 ° C. Grease a large baking dish with coconut oil.
- Combine coconut sugar, vanilla, and nutmeg in a small bowl.

- Place about ⅓ of the peaches in a prepared baking dish. Sprinkle with ⅓ of the coconut sugar mixture. Repeat the layers two more times.
- Bake in preheated oven for 30 minutes. Pour water over the peaches and continue cooking until tender, another 15 minutes.

NUTRITION FACTS (PER SERVING)		
Calories	94	
Total Fat	1.2g	2%
Saturated Fat	0.6g	3%
Cholesterol	0mg	0%
Sodium	10mg	0%
Total Carbohydrate	20g	7%
Dietary Fiber	2.4g	9%
Total Sugars	15.2g	
Protein	1.7g	

Tips: Peaches are not a quick fix for weight loss, but they can help you shed extra pounds! They make a great low-calorie snack, and adding them to oatmeal or pancakes will make your healthy breakfast all the more delicious.

Zucchini Cookies

| Prep time: 15 min | Cook time: 10 min | Servings: 18 |

Ingredients

- ¼ cup butter, softened
- ½ cup coconut sugar
- 1 egg
- ½ cup grated zucchini
- 1 cup whole wheat flour
- ½ tsp baking soda
- ¼ tsp salt
- ½ tsp ground nutmeg
- ¼ tsp ground cinnamon
- ½ cup apricots

Instructions

- In a medium bowl, combine butter and coconut sugar.

- Stir until smooth.
- Beat the egg, then add the zucchini. Mix together the flour, nutmeg, salt and baking powder. Stir in the zucchini mixture. Add the apricots.
- Cover the dough and refrigerate for at least 1 hour.
- Preheat the oven to 190 ° C. Grease the baking sheets. Use the tsp to drop the dough onto the prepared baking sheet. The cookies should be spaced about 2 cm apart.
- Bake in the oven for 8 to 10 minutes until firm. Let cookies cool slightly on baking sheets before placing them on wire racks to cool completely.

NUTRITION FACTS (PER SERVING)

Calories	57	
Total Fat	2.9g	4%
Saturated Fat	1.7g	9%
Cholesterol	16mg	5%
Sodium	90mg	4%
Total Carbohydrate	6.5g	2%
Dietary Fiber	0.3g	1%
Total Sugars	0.5g	
Protein	1.2g	

Tips: Egg white brings strength, stability and humidity. The yolk, where all the fat in an egg is found, adds richness, tenderness and taste. So, if you lay an extra egg, you will end up with a harder cookie.

Yummy Red Dragon Fruit Sorbet

| Prep time: 10 min | Cook time: 5 min | Servings: 4 |

Ingredients

- ½ cup maple syrup
- ¼ cup water
- ⅛ cup lime juice
- 1-½ cups cubed Red dragon fruit

Instructions

- Combine maple syrup, water and lime juice in a saucepan over medium heat; cook, about 5 minutes.
- Remove from the heat and refrigerate for about 30 minutes.

- Puree the red dragon fruit in a blender or food processor.
- Add the mashed red dragon fruit to the syrup mixture. Transfer the red dragon fruit mixture to an ice cream maker and freeze according to the manufacturer's instructions.

NUTRITION FACTS (PER SERVING)

Calories	116	
Total Fat	0.1g	0%
Saturated Fat	0g	0%
Cholesterol	0mg	0%
Sodium	5mg	0%
Total Carbohydrate	30g	11%
Dietary Fiber	0.3g	1%
Total Sugars	26.5g	
Protein	0.1g	

Tips: Dragon fruit is a low-calorie fruit that contains less sugar and fewer carbs than many other tropical fruits.

Papaya and Mint Sorbet

| Prep time: 10 min | Cook time: 0 min | Servings: 8 |

Ingredients

- 1 papaya - peeled, cored, and cut into chunks
- ¼ cup coconut sugar
- ¼ cup pineapple juice
- ⅛ cup mint leaves

Instructions

- Combine the papaya, coconut sugar, pineapple juice and mint in a blender until smooth.
- Chill for 1 hour in the refrigerator.

- Place the mixture in an ice maker and mix it according to the manufacturer's instructions.
- Store in an airtight container and freeze for 8 hours or overnight.

NUTRITION FACTS (PER SERVING)		
Calories	25	
Total Fat	0.1g	0%
Saturated Fat	0g	0%
Cholesterol	0mg	0%
Sodium	5mg	0%
Total Carbohydrate	6g	2%
Dietary Fiber	0.8g	3%
Total Sugars	3.9g	
Protein	0.3g	

Tips: Glucose syrup, corn syrup, or invert sugar can improve the texture of the final sherbet.

Butternut Squash Pie

| Prep time: 10 min | Cook time: 20 min | Servings: 18 |

Ingredients

- *1 cup whole wheat flour*
- *½ cup coconut sugar*
- *½ tsp baking powder*
- *½ tsp baking soda*
- *¼ tsp ground cinnamon*
- *⅛ tsp ground cloves*
- *⅛ tsp ground ginger*
- *⅛ tsp ground nutmeg*
- *⅛ tsp salt*
- *½ (15 ounces) can Butternut Squash puree*
- *⅛ cup coconut oil*

- ½ tbsp vanilla extract

Instructions

- Preheat the oven to 190° C. Lightly grease a 9-inch square baking dish or lay parchment paper.
- Sift the flour, coconut sugar, baking powder, baking powder, cinnamon, cloves, ginger, nutmeg and salt in a bowl. Stir the Butternut Squash puree, coconut oil and vanilla extract into the flour mixture until a thick paste form. Beat in a prepared baking dish.
- Bake for 20 minutes. You can check if ready by inserting a toothpick in the center of the cake. It should come out clean, otherwise bake for further 5 min.

NUTRITION FACTS (PER SERVING)

Calories	44	
Total Fat	1.6g	2%
Saturated Fat	1.3g	7%
Cholesterol	0mg	0%
Sodium	53mg	2%
Total Carbohydrate	6.4g	2%
Dietary Fiber	0.3g	1%
Total Sugars	0.4g	
Protein	0.8g	

Tips: Butternut squash is an excellent source of many vitamins and minerals.

Banana Oat Bars

| Prep time: 5 min | Cook time: 35 min | Servings: 10 |

Ingredients

- 1 cup quick cooking oats
- ¼ cup honey
- 1 tsp baking powder
- ½ tsp ground cinnamon
- ¼ tsp baking soda
- ¼ cup apricots
- ½ cup mashed bananas
- ⅛ cup almond milk
- 1 egg whites

- ½ tsp vanilla extract

Instructions

- Preheat the oven to 175 ° C.
- Mix the dry ingredients in one bowl.
- Combine the bananas, honey, egg whites, vanilla and milk in the separate bowl.
- Mix all the ingredients from both bowls well together.
- Bake in 9x13-inch pan sprayed with nonstick spray for about 35 minutes.
- Cut into bars when cool.
- Garnish with cinnamon and sugar and serve.

NUTRITION FACTS (PER SERVING)

Calories	58	
Total Fat	1g	1%
Saturated Fat	0.5g	2%
Cholesterol	0mg	0%
Sodium	19mg	1%
Total Carbohydrate	11.1g	4%
Dietary Fiber	1.2g	4%
Total Sugars	4.7g	
Protein	1.8g	

Tips: Bananas are full of potassium, an electrolyte mineral that allows electricity to flow through the body to make the heartbeat.

Orange Sesame Seed Biscotti

| Prep time: 5 min | Cook time: 35 min | Servings: 18 |

Ingredients

- *1 cup whole wheat flour*
- *½ cup coconut sugar*
- *¼ cup finely ground walnuts*
- *¼ tsp baking powder*
- *¼ tsp baking soda*
- *½ tbsp orange zest*
- *1-½ tbsp sesame seeds*
- *1 egg*
- *½ tsp orange extract*

Instructions

- Preheat the oven to 175 ° C.

- Line a baking sheet with parchment paper.
- Combine the whole wheat flour, coconut sugar, ground walnuts, baking powder and baking powder.
- Combine the orange zest, sesame seeds, egg, and orange extract. Add the dry mixture and mix well. Shape the dough into 2 stems and place on a baking sheet.
- Bake at 175 ° C for 30 minutes. Let cool slightly and cut diagonally into ½-inch slices. Bake the slices for an additional 8 to 10 minutes until dry.
- Let cool completely before consuming or store for later.

NUTRITION FACTS (PER SERVING)

Calories	46	
Total Fat	1.6g	2%
Saturated Fat	0.2g	1%
Cholesterol	9mg	3%
Sodium	21mg	1%
Total Carbohydrate	6.2g	2%
Dietary Fiber	0.4g	1%
Total Sugars	0.1g	
Protein	1.6g	

Tips: Sesame seeds contain many important trace minerals and macro minerals, as well as healthy fats.

Gingerbread Balls

| Prep time: 10 min | Cook time: 0 min | Servings: 10 |

Ingredients

- ½ cup gluten-free rolled oats
- ¼ cup all-purpose flour
- ½ tbsp ground cinnamon
- ½ tsp ground ginger
- ¼ tsp ground nutmeg
- ¼ tsp vanilla extract
- 1 cup figs, pitted and chopped
- 1-½ tbsp powdered white sugar

Instructions

- Put the oatmeal, all-purpose flour, cinnamon, ginger, nutmeg and vanilla extract in a blender.
- Stir well, until smooth. Mix the dates in batches until a smooth paste form.
- Form 1-inch balls and roll in the powdered white sugar.

NUTRITION FACTS (PER SERVING)

Calories	40	
Total Fat	0.4g	1%
Saturated Fat	0g	0%
Cholesterol	0mg	0%
Sodium	0mg	0%
Total Carbohydrate	8.4g	3%
Dietary Fiber	1g	3%
Total Sugars	2.3g	
Protein	1.1g	

Tips: Figs are rich in natural sugars, minerals and soluble fiber. For example, they are rich in minerals such as potassium, iron calcium, copper and magnesium. Figs are also a great source of many vitamins, such as A and K and are therefore very good for your health.

SMOOTHIES AND DRINKS

Mango Ginger Smoothie

| Prep time: 5 min | Cook time: 0 min | Servings: 2 |

Ingredients

- *1 cup cooked lentils cooled*
- *2 cups frozen mango chunks*
- *1-½ cups orange juice*
- *2 tsp chopped fresh ginger*
- *2 tsp maple syrup (optional)*
- *Pinch of ground nutmeg, plus more for garnish*
- *6 ice cubes*

Instructions

- Put the lentils, mango, orange juice, ginger, maple syrup, nutmeg and ice cubes in a blender.
- Beat over high heat for 2 to 3 minutes until smooth.
- Garnish with more nutmeg if desired.

NUTRITION FACTS (PER SERVING)

Calories	292	
Total Fat	1.4g	2%
Saturated Fat	0.3g	2%
Cholesterol	0mg	0%
Sodium	239mg	10%
Total Carbohydrate	62.8g	23%
Dietary Fiber	11g	39%
Total Sugars	38.8g	
Protein	11.3g	

Tips: Cooking red lentils: Cook in boiling water for about 15 minutes until tender. Drain and cool. (1 dry cup = 2 ½ cups cooked). You can freeze the smoothie in ½ cup portions for up to 3 months (thaw before use).

Kiwi Strawberry Banana Smoothie

| Prep time: 5 min | Cook time: 0 min | Servings: 4 |

Ingredients

- 2 cups sliced fresh strawberries
- 1 small banana, sliced
- ½ (6 ounces) container low fat Greek yogurt
- 1 cup ice cubes
- ½ kiwi fruit, peeled and sliced

Instructions

- In a blender, combine all ingredients.
- Cover and blend until smooth.

NUTRITION FACTS (PER SERVING)		
Calories	70	
Total Fat	0.9g	1%
Saturated Fat	0.4g	2%
Cholesterol	1mg	0%
Sodium	11mg	0%
Total Carbohydrate	13.7g	5%
Dietary Fiber	2.4g	9%
Total Sugars	8.5g	
Protein	3.4g	

Tips: Strawberries are bright red, juicy and sweet. They're a great source of vitamin C and manganese, and they also contain decent amounts of folic acid (vitamin B9) and potassium.

Berry Mint Smoothie

| Prep time: 5 min | Cook time: 0 min | Servings: 4 |

Ingredients

- *1 cup low-fat plain yogurt*
- *½ cup coconut milk*
- *2 cups frozen mixed berries*
- *½ cup lime juice*
- *1-2 tbsp fresh mint*
- *1 tbsp honey (optional)*

Instructions

- In a blender, combine yogurt, milk, mixed berries, lime juice, fresh mint and honey, if used.
- Cover and blend until smooth.

NUTRITION FACTS (PER SERVING)

Calories	168	
Total Fat	8.2g	10%
Saturated Fat	7g	35%
Cholesterol	4mg	1%
Sodium	48mg	2%
Total Carbohydrate	18.4g	7%
Dietary Fiber	3.3g	12%
Total Sugars	13.4g	
Protein	4.8g	

Tips: Packed with antioxidants and Phyto flavonoids, these berries are also high in potassium and vitamin C, making them a top choice for doctors and nutritionists. They lower your risk of cancer and heart disease and are also anti-inflammatory.

Banana Protein Smoothie

| Prep time: 5 min | Cook time: 0 min | Servings: 4 |

Ingredients

- 1 banana, frozen
- 1 scoop vanilla protein powder
- ½ cup coconut milk
- 2 tsp unsweetened cocoa powder
- 1 tsp honey (optional)

Instructions

- In a blender, combine banana, milk, vanilla protein powder, cocoa powder and honey.

- Cover and blend until smooth.

NUTRITION FACTS (PER SERVING)		
Calories	307	
Total Fat	3.5g	4%
Saturated Fat	2g	10%
Cholesterol	12mg	4%
Sodium	113mg	5%
Total Carbohydrate	41.2g	15%
Dietary Fiber	4.8g	17%
Total Sugars	26g	
Protein	33g	

Tips: Bananas are also loaded with calcium, magnesium, zinc, and vitamins A, B6, B12, fiber, and folic acid, which are essential vitamins and nutrients that help babies gain healthy weight.

Kale and Chia Seed Green Smoothie

| Prep time: 5 min | Cook time: 0 min | Servings: 1 |

Ingredients

- *1 small ripe banana*
- *½ green apple, peeled if desired, chopped*
- *1 cup chopped kale leaves; tough stems removed*
- *¼ cup cold lime juice*
- *¼ cup cold water*
- *ice cubes*
- *½ tbsp ground chia seeds*

Instructions

- In a blender, combine banana, green apple, kale, ice cube, lime juice, water and chia seeds.
- Cover and blend until smooth.

NUTRITION FACTS (PER SERVING)

Calories   184
Total Fat 0.5g   1%
Saturated Fat 0.1g   1%
Cholesterol 0mg   0%
Sodium 33mg   1%
Total Carbohydrate 46.4g   17%
Dietary Fiber 6.4g   23%
Total Sugars 24.1g
Protein 3.4g

Tips: Kale is a warrior who fights heart disease, cancer, inflammation, and toxins. To get the most out of what's on offer, eat 1 ½ cups several times a week. At 33 calories per cup, that's a really big investment in nutrition.

Banana Cauliflower Smoothie

| Prep time: 5 min | Cook time: 0 min | Servings: 1 |

Ingredients

- ½ cup frozen riced cauliflower
- ¼ cup frozen mixed berries
- ½ cup sliced frozen banana
- 1 cup unsweetened coconut milk
- 1 tsp honey (optional)

Instructions

- In a blender, combine riced cauliflower, mixed berries, banana, coconut milk and honey.
- Cover and blend until smooth.

NUTRITION FACTS (PER SERVING)

Calories	168	
Total Fat	4.4g	6%
Saturated Fat	4.1g	20%
Cholesterol	0mg	0%
Sodium	49mg	2%
Total Carbohydrate	31.7g	12%
Dietary Fiber	5.2g	19%
Total Sugars	18.4g	
Protein	2.1g	

Tips: Coconut milk is a versatile ingredient and a great alternative to milk. Like other coconut products, it may offer various health benefits.

Pineapple Smoothie

| Prep time: 5 min | Cook time: 0 min | Servings: 1 |

Ingredients

- ½ cup fresh or drained canned pineapple
- ⅛ cup orange juice
- ¼ cup plain yogurt
- ⅛ cup water
- 2 ice cubes, crushed

Instructions

- In a blender, combine pineapple, orange juice, plain yogurt, water and ice cubes.
- Cover and blend until smooth.

NUTRITION FACTS (PER SERVING)

Calories	99	
Total Fat	0.9g	1%
Saturated Fat	0.6g	3%
Cholesterol	4mg	1%
Sodium	44mg	2%
Total Carbohydrate	18.4g	7%
Dietary Fiber	1.2g	4%
Total Sugars	15g	
Protein	4.1g	

Tips: pineapple may be particularly beneficial for women because its high content of vitamin C plays an important role in supporting bone health and reducing the risk of osteoporosis. Additionally, pineapple provides nutrients like copper and several B vitamins that are important during pregnancy.

Strawberry Raspberry Smoothie

| Prep time: 5 min | Cook time: 0 min | Servings: 2 |

Ingredients

- *½ (6 ounces) container plain yogurt*
- *½ cup almond milk*
- *¾ cups fresh sliced strawberries*
- *¼ cup fresh red raspberries*
- *½ ice cubes, crushed*

Instructions

- In a blender, combine plain yogurt, almond milk, strawberry, raspberry and ice cubes.
- Cover and blend until smooth.

NUTRITION FACTS (PER SERVING)		
Calories	98	
Total Fat	1.9g	2%
Saturated Fat	0.7g	4%
Cholesterol	3mg	1%
Sodium	71mg	3%
Total Carbohydrate	13.7g	5%
Dietary Fiber	1.9g	7%
Total Sugars	9.9g	
Protein	5.8g	

Tips: Berries are high in potassium and vitamin C. They can lower your risk of cancer and heart disease and are also anti-inflammatory.

Green Tea Peach Smoothie

| Prep time: 5 min | Cook time: 0 min | Servings: 1 |

Ingredients

- 1 cup frozen peaches
- ½ cup cold unsweetened green tea
- ½ tbsp maple syrup
- ½ tbsp lime juice

Instructions

- In a blender, combine peaches, green tea, maple syrup and lime juice.
- Cover and blend until smooth.

NUTRITION FACTS (PER SERVING)		
Calories	91	
Total Fat	0.4g	1%
Saturated Fat	0g	0%
Cholesterol	0mg	0%
Sodium	1mg	0%
Total Carbohydrate	22.6g	8%
Dietary Fiber	2.4g	9%
Total Sugars	20.3g	
Protein	1.5g	

Tips: Green tea has been shown to improve blood circulation and lower cholesterol levels. A 2013 review of numerous studies found that green tea helped prevent a variety of heart problems, from high blood pressure to heart failure.

Mermaid Smoothie Bowl

| Prep time: 5 min | Cook time: 0 min | Servings: 1 |

Ingredients

- *1 frozen banana, peeled*
- *1 kiwi, peeled*
- *½ cup fresh pineapple chunks*
- *½ cup unsweetened coconut milk*
- *1 tsp spirulina powder*
- *¼ cup fresh blueberries*
- *¼ tbsp almond sliced*
- *¼ small Fuji apple*

Instructions

- Slice the apple into pieces.
- In a blender, combine banana, kiwi, pineapple, coconut milk and spirulina powder.
- Cover and blend until smooth.
- Pour the smoothie into the bowl
- Top with blueberries and apples.

NUTRITION FACTS (PER SERVING)		
Calories	339	
Total Fat	9.1g	12%
Saturated Fat	4.5g	22%
Cholesterol	0mg	0%
Sodium	30mg	1%
Total Carbohydrate	65.9g	24%
Dietary Fiber	10.8g	39%
Total Sugars	39.1g	
Protein	5.9g	

Tips: Add a variety of fruits or vegetables in a variety of textures.

Spinach Protein Smoothie

| Prep time: 5 min | Cook time: 0 min | Servings: 1 |

Ingredients

- *½ cup soy milk*
- *1 cup frozen green grapes*
- *1 cup baby spinach*
- *1 tsp maple syrup*
- *1 scoop protein powder*
- *3 ice cubes*

Instructions

- In a blender, combine soy milk, green grapes, spinach, maple syrup, ice cubes and protein powder.
- Cover and blend until smooth.

NUTRITION FACTS (PER SERVING)		
Calories	300	
Total Fat	4.1g	5%
Saturated Fat	1.2g	6%
Cholesterol	65mg	22%
Sodium	157mg	7%
Total Carbohydrate	39.9g	15%
Dietary Fiber	2.4g	9%
Total Sugars	29.9g	
Protein	27g	

Tips: Spinach is also one of the best dietary sources of magnesium, which is necessary for energy metabolism, maintenance of muscle and nerve functions, a regular heart rate, a healthy immune system, and maintenance of blood pressure. Magnesium is also involved in hundreds of other biochemical reactions that take place in the body.

Pumpkin and Pear Smoothie

| Prep time: 5 min | Cook time: 0 min | Servings: 2 |

Ingredients

- ¾ cup soy milk
- 1 cup chopped apples (2 medium)
- ¼ (15 ounces) can pumpkin
- 1 tbsp plain yogurt
- ½ cup ice
- 1 tbsp honey
- ⅛ tsp pumpkin pie spice
- pinch salt
- 1 scoop vanilla protein powder

Instructions

- In a blender, combine soy milk, apple, pumpkin, plain yogurt, ice cubes, honey, pumpkin pie salt and protein powder.
- Cover and blend until smooth.

NUTRITION FACTS (PER SERVING)

Calories	206	
Total Fat	2.3g	3%
Saturated Fat	0.3g	2%
Cholesterol	5mg	2%
Sodium	165mg	7%
Total Carbohydrate	33.9g	12%
Dietary Fiber	4.2g	15%
Total Sugars	26g	
Protein	15.6g	

Tips: Your body uses beta-carotene and converts it into vitamin A, which is important for eye health. Vitamin A supports the retina and absorbs light. With just one cup of pumpkin, you get over 200% of the recommended daily intake of vitamin A.

Cucumber Breeze Smoothie

| Prep time: 5 min | Cook time: 0 min | Servings: 1 |

Ingredients

- 1 small cucumber, chopped
- 2 sliced Dragon fruit, peeled
- ½ cup ginger
- ¼ cup plain yogurt
- 1 tbsp fresh mint leaves
- 6 ice cubes

Instructions

- In a blender, combine cucumber, dragon fruit, ginger, plain yogurt and fresh mint.
- Cover and blend until smooth.

NUTRITION FACTS (PER SERVING)

Calories	242	
Total Fat	3.7g	5%
Saturated Fat	1.6g	8%
Cholesterol	4mg	1%
Sodium	64mg	3%
Total Carbohydrate	46.5g	17%
Dietary Fiber	7.3g	26%
Total Sugars	10.9g	
Protein	9.6g	

Tips: Cucumbers contain magnesium, potassium and vitamin K. These 3 nutrients are essential for the proper functioning of the cardiovascular system. Taking magnesium and potassium can lower your blood pressure.

Blueberry Banana Smoothies

| Prep time: 5 min | Cook time: 0 min | Servings: 2 |

Ingredients

- ¾ cups frozen unsweetened sweet cherries
- ½ cup unsweetened coconut milk
- ½ cup yogurt
- ¼ cup fresh or frozen unsweetened blueberries
- ½ small banana, peeled

Instructions

- In a blender, combine cherries, coconut milk, yogurt, blueberries and banana.
- Cover and blend until smooth.

NUTRITION FACTS (PER SERVING)

Calories	99	
Total Fat	2.1g	3%
Saturated Fat	1.6g	8%
Cholesterol	4mg	1%
Sodium	43mg	2%
Total Carbohydrate	21.5g	8%
Dietary Fiber	2.5g	9%
Total Sugars	16g	
Protein	4.3g	

Tips: A bowl of blueberries can boost immunity and lower your risk of diabetes, obesity, and heart disease.

Pomegranate Blackberry Smoothie

| Prep time: 5 min | Cook time: 0 min | Servings: 1 |

Ingredients

- 1cup frozen mixed berries
- ½ cup pomegranate juice
- 1 small banana
- ¼ cup tofu
- ½ cup water

Instructions

- In a blender, combine mixed berries, pomegranate juice, banana, tofu and water.
- Cover and blend until smooth.

NUTRITION FACTS (PER SERVING)

Calories	289	
Total Fat	3.5g	4%
Saturated Fat	0.7g	3%
Cholesterol	0mg	0%
Sodium	17mg	1%
Total Carbohydrate	59.6g	22%
Dietary Fiber	8.2g	29%
Total Sugars	38.7g	
Protein	7.3g	

Tips: Regular consumption of pomegranate improves gut health, digestion, and keeps bowel disease at bay.

Green Monster

| Prep time: 5 min | Cook time: 0 min | Servings: 1 |

Ingredients

- ¼ cup pineapple juice
- ¼ cup water
- ½ scoop plant-based vanilla protein powder
- ½ peaches, chopped
- ½ cup baby kale, loosely packed
- ½ frozen banana
- ¼ ripe avocado

Instructions

- In a blender, add pineapple juice, water, protein powder, peaches, kale banana and avocado.
- Cover and blend until smooth.

NUTRITION FACTS (PER SERVING)		
Calories	289	
Total Fat	11.4g	15%
Saturated Fat	2.1g	11%
Cholesterol	0mg	0%
Sodium	210mg	9%
Total Carbohydrate	37.1g	13%
Dietary Fiber	6.7g	24%
Total Sugars	20.7g	
Protein	13.8g	

Tips: Avocados are an excellent source of vitamins C, E, K, and B-6, as well as riboflavin, niacin, folic acid, pantothenic acid, magnesium, and potassium. They even contain lutein, beta-carotene, and omega-3 fatty acids.

Cranberry Ginger Smoothie

| Prep time: 5 min | Cook time: 0 min | Servings: 1 |

Ingredients

- *½ cup cranberries fresh or frozen*
- *¼ tsp ginger minced*
- *1 tsp maple syrup*
- *½ cup coconut water*

- *½ cup water*
- *handful ice*

Instructions

- In a blender, add cranberries, ginger, maple syrup, coconut water, water and ice.
- Cover and blend until smooth.

NUTRITION FACTS (PER SERVING)		
Calories	105	
Total Fat	0.3g	0%
Saturated Fat	0.2g	1%
Cholesterol	0mg	0%
Sodium	128mg	6%
Total Carbohydrate	22.9g	8%
Dietary Fiber	3.3g	12%
Total Sugars	17g	
Protein	0.9g	

Tips: Many people consider blueberries to be a superfood because of their high levels of nutrients and antioxidants. In fact, research has linked the nutrients in blueberries to the risk of urinary tract infections (UTIs), the prevention of certain cancers, improved immune function and lowered blood pressure.

Almond Apple Smoothie

| Prep time: 5 min | Cook time: 0 min | Servings: 1 |

Ingredients

- ½ cup unsweetened almond milk
- 1 cup apple slices, peeled, or skin on
- ¼ tsp ground ginger
- handful ice cubes
- A little maple syrup (optional)

Instructions

- In a blender, add almond milk, ginger, maple syrup, apple, water and ice.
- Cover and blend until smooth.

NUTRITION FACTS (PER SERVING)

Calories	101	
Total Fat	1.8g	2%
Saturated Fat	0.2g	1%
Cholesterol	0mg	0%
Sodium	90mg	4%
Total Carbohydrate	23.2g	8%
Dietary Fiber	5.5g	20%
Total Sugars	17g	
Protein	0.5g	

Tips: Every time you eat an apple, you get a good dose of this important vitamin. B-complex vitamins are also found in apples. These include riboflavin, thiamine, and vitamin B-6, all of which are essential for maintaining red blood cells and maintaining a strong and healthy nervous system. Apples also contain vitamin K.

Citrus Tangy Boosting Smoothie

| Prep time: 5 min | Cook time: 0 min | Servings: 1 |

Ingredients

- ½ orange peeled and chopped, seeds removed
- ½ lemon peeled and chopped, seeds removed
- A few kale leaves
- 1 parsnip peeled and chopped (or grated)
- ¾ cup coconut milk
- ½ apple peeled and chopped

Instructions

- In a blender, add coconut milk, oranges, lemon apple, kale, parsnip, and apple.

- Cover and blend until smooth.

NUTRITION FACTS (PER SERVING)

Calories	294	
Total Fat	9.8g	13%
Saturated Fat	7.6g	38%
Cholesterol	0mg	0%
Sodium	39mg	2%
Total Carbohydrate	52.6g	19%
Dietary Fiber	11.7g	42%
Total Sugars	24.8g	
Protein	4.1g	

Tips: Research suggests that these citrus phytochemicals help the body and protect us against diseases such as heart disease and cancer. They are also believed to have anti-inflammatory, antiviral, and antimicrobial benefits. Oranges are also a great source of fiber, B vitamins, vitamin A, calcium, and potassium.

Vanilla Peach Avocado Smoothie

| Prep time: 5 min | Cook time: 0 min | Servings: 1 |

Ingredients

- *½ cup fresh or frozen peach slices*
- *1 cup water*
- *¼ avocado peeled*
- *½ tsp vanilla extract*
- *handful ice*

Instructions

- In a blender, add peaches, water, avocado, vanilla extract and ice.
- Cover and blend until smooth.

NUTRITION FACTS (PER SERVING)

Calories	103	
Total Fat	6.7g	9%
Saturated Fat	0.9g	5%
Cholesterol	0mg	0%
Sodium	11mg	0%
Total Carbohydrate	10.5g	4%
Dietary Fiber	4g	14%
Total Sugars	4.9g	
Protein	0.9g	

<u>Tips: Peaches are not a quick fix for weight loss, but they can help you shed extra pounds! They make a great low-calorie snack, and adding them to oatmeal or pancakes will make your healthy breakfast all the more delicious.</u>

Immunity Boosting Smoothie

| Prep time: 5 min | Cook time: 0 min | Servings: 2 |

Ingredients

- ⅛ cup blueberries
- large strawberries hulled
- ½ small peaches cored
- ½ tbsp honey
- ⅛ cup dried cranberries
- ¾ cups water to taste

Instructions

- Put everything in a blender, cover and blend until smooth.

NUTRITION FACTS (PER SERVING)		
Calories	45	
Total Fat	0.2g	0%
Saturated Fat	0g	0%
Cholesterol	0mg	0%
Sodium	0mg	0%
Total Carbohydrate	11.2g	4%
Dietary Fiber	1.4g	5%
Total Sugars	9.8g	
Protein	0.6g	

Tips: Add a pinch or two of chia seeds after you blend for a nice texture variation and a little mid-day energy boost.

Apple Cucumber Refresher

| Prep time: 5 min | Cook time: 0 min | Servings: 1 |

Ingredients

- *½ cup apple juice*
- *1 small banana*

- *½ English cucumber peeled and chopped*
- *Juice from half a lemon*
- *basil leaves torn*
- *1 handful ice cubes*

Instructions

- Put everything in a blender.
- Cover and blend until smooth.

NUTRITION FACTS (PER SERVING)

Calories	170	
Total Fat	0.7g	1%
Saturated Fat	0.2g	1%
Cholesterol	0mg	0%
Sodium	7mg	0%
Total Carbohydrate	43.6g	16%
Dietary Fiber	5.1g	18%
Total Sugars	26.3g	
Protein	2.5g	

<u>Tips: Find a smoothie recipe that you will love to drink all week, buy the ingredients in bulk, do it all in one sitting, and your smoothie drinking days will be much easier.</u>

Blueberry- Carrots Smoothie

| Prep time: 5 min | Cook time: 0 min | Servings: 1 |

Ingredients

- 1 Carrot finely chopped
- ½ cup blueberries fresh or frozen
- ¾ cups coconut milk
- handful ice

Instructions

- Put everything in a blender, cover and blend until smooth.

NUTRITION FACTS (PER SERVING)

Calories	160	
Total Fat	9.3g	12%
Saturated Fat	7.5g	37%
Cholesterol	0mg	0%
Sodium	64mg	3%
Total Carbohydrate	18.7g	7%
Dietary Fiber	3.3g	12%
Total Sugars	10.2g	
Protein	2.1g	

Tips: Keep it simple with three ingredients and a simple freezer hack that will make sure you get them ready.

Beet and Strawberry Smoothie

| Prep time: 5 min | Cook time: 0 min | Servings: 1 |

Ingredients

- *2 beets cooked and peeled*
- *1 cup unsweetened almond milk*
- *1 cup frozen strawberry*
- *½ lemon juiced*

Instructions

- In a blender, add beet, almond milk, strawberries and lemon.
- Blend until smooth.

NUTRITION FACTS (PER SERVING)		
Calories	173	
Total Fat	3.9g	5%
Saturated Fat	0.4g	2%
Cholesterol	0mg	0%
Sodium	312mg	14%
Total Carbohydrate	34.6g	13%
Dietary Fiber	8.2g	29%
Total Sugars	23.2g	
Protein	4.2g	

Tips: make your own smoothie every day with an easy-to-clean portable blender.

Watermelon Smoothie

| Prep time: 5 min | Cook time: 0 min | Servings: 1 |

Ingredients

- *1 cup seedless watermelon chopped*
- *½ cup strawberries*
- *½ cup Greek yogurt*
- *handful ice*

Instructions

- In a blender, add watermelon, strawberries, Greek yogurt and ice.
- Cover and blend until smooth.

NUTRITION FACTS (PER SERVING)

Calories	134	
Total Fat	2.2g	3%
Saturated Fat	1.5g	8%
Cholesterol	5mg	2%
Sodium	33mg	1%
Total Carbohydrate	19.1g	7%
Dietary Fiber	1.9g	7%
Total Sugars	17.1g	
Protein	11.1g	

Tips: Rely on bananas whenever you need a natural thickener and sweetener. Bananas are one of the best smoothie ingredients ever!

RECOVERY RECIPES

Homemade Chicken Broth

| Prep time: 15 min | Cook time: 4 h 30 min | Servings: several |

Ingredients

- *Meat of 1 organic chicken (2-3 kg), skinless and boneless*
- *4 carrots*
- *3 celery ribs*
- *1-2 onions*
- *Half a leek*
- *4 bay leaves*
- *Hand full of thyme*
- *Hand full of parsley*
- *2 tbsp of peppercorns*
- *Salt and ground black pepper*

Instructions

- Preheat the oven to 428 degrees F and put some parchment paper onto a baking tray.
- Remove the giblets out of the chicken (if any) and place them onto a baking tray. You can leave it whole or cut it in into pieces.
- Add whole carrots, roughly chopped onions, leeks and celery.
- Season with salt and pepper and put in the oven for 20-30 minutes, until it is a bit brown (or burnt) on the outside. This will give a broth a great taste.
- Put out of the oven and put all the ingredients into a medium-sized pot and cover with water. Season with bay leaves, peppercorns, thyme and parsley, then bring to a boil.
- Lower to medium heat, put the lid on and simmer for 4 hours.
- After it is done, remove the chicken and all the veggies from the pot. You can shred and use the meat if you'd like, but the chicken is pretty overcooked and might not be tasty.
- Strain the broth until it's clean of seasoning and all the veggies.
- To eliminate the fat, let the broth cool overnight or for a few hours in the refrigerator.
- A light-yellow cover will form on the top of the broth – carefully remove it and discard it.

Tips: You can portion off quantities in containers, glass jars or Ziplock bags to keep in the refrigerator or freezer for future use. You can keep it in the fridge for up to 5-7 days and in the freezer for several weeks.

Homemade Vegetable Stock

| Prep time: 15 min | Cook time: 4 h 20 min | Servings: several |

Ingredients

- *3 carrots*
- *2 stalks of celery*
- *1 onion*
- *A handful of mushrooms*
- *½ leek*
- *1 cup kale*
- *1 cup kohlrabi*
- *1-2 tsp sea salt*
- *1 sprig of parsley,*
- *1 sprig of rosemary,*
- *4 bay leaves*

- *1 sprig of thyme*
- *1 tsp peppercorns*
- *1 tsp tomato paste*
- *10 cups water*

Instructions

- Clean your veggies well, under warm water. Chop into smaller pieces (peels on).
- Preheat the oven to 400 degrees F and put some parchment paper onto a baking tray.
- Place all the veggies onto a baking tray and bake for 15-20 minutes or until a bit brown (or burnt) on the outside.
- Put off the oven and put all the ingredients into a medium-sized pot and cover with water. Season with salt, bay leaves, peppercorns, thyme, rosemary, parsley and tomato paste, then bring to a boil.
- Reduce the heat to simmer and put the lead on. Stir occasionally.
- Cook for a further 1h. Taste and adjust the flavors along if needed (add in some more salt or herbs, etc.).
- Once done, leave the broth to cool for a bit, then strain the broth, to remove all the solid parts and discard them.
- Enjoy immediately and save for later.

Tips: if desired, you can use other vegetables for cooking the broth too, like tomatoes, celery root, potatoes, a few pieces of pumpkin or zucchini, or use vegetable scraps and peels. You can cut veggies into thin pieces or strips (with a peeler), which will help your broth to develop more flavor.

Celery Juice

| Prep time: 5 min | Cook time: 0 min | Servings: 1 |

Ingredients

- *1 bunch of celery*
- *1 pinch of grated ginger*
- *Water*

Instructions

- Wash and cut up the celery to 1-inch pieces or less, and put into a blender, along with ginger.
- Add ¼ cup of water and blend until smooth.
- Strain the juice through a strainer or a strainer or thin cotton cloth or filter. Discard the solid parts.
- If you don't drink it immediately you can keep in the fridge for up to 2 days.

Tips: Celery is great for your gut. It is one of the best antioxidants, low in calories, a good source of magnesium and is highly nutritious. To spice this juice up, you can also add a few mint leaves into the mix.

Carrot Juice

| Prep time: 5 min | Cook time: 0 min | Servings: 1 |

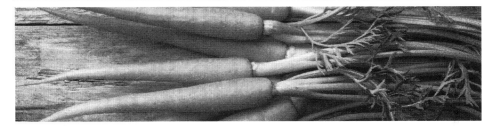

Ingredients

- *5 carrots*
- *Water*

Instructions

- Wash and cut up the carrots to 1-inch pieces or less, then blanch in boiling water for 2-3 min.
- Chill the carrots and put them into a blender. Add half a cup of water and put the lid on the blender. Blend until smooth.
- Strain the juice through a strainer or a strainer or thin cotton cloth or filter. Discard the solid parts.
- Drink the liquid immediately or keep it in the fridge for up to 2 days.

Tips: Carrot juice contains a lot of vitamins and minerals and is highly nutritious. It helps with many symptoms and conditions, among others with digestion and acidity troubles. It can improve your eye health, skin health, heart health and boost your immunity.

Fruit and Vegetable Drink

| Prep time: 5 min | Cook time: 0 min | Servings: 2 |

Ingredients

- *1 carrot*
- *A few pieces of celery*
- *A small piece of kohlrabi*
- *1 mango*
- *1 peach*
- *1 nectarine*
- *A few parsley and lemon mint strings;*
- *0% fat yogurt or milk or kefir*

Instructions

- Wash and peel all the veggies and fruit.
- Chop the fruit and veggies into smaller pieces, then put them into a blender.
- Blend for a minute or until smooth.
- Strain the juice through a strainer or a strainer or thin cotton cloth or filter. Discard the solid parts.
- Transfer to a glass and garnish with some lemon mint leaves or a drizzle of honey.

Warm Apple Juice

| Prep time: 10 min | Cook time: 20 min | Servings: several |

Ingredients

- *2 kg ripe apples (pilled and cleaned)*
- *8 l of water*
- *1-2 cups of sugar (or to taste)*
- *A pinch of cinnamon (optional)*

Instructions

- Wash and clean the apples, remove the seeds and peels and discard them. Cut into smaller pieces.
- Put a large cooking pot on the stow, add in the apples and add approx. 2 l of water, to cover all apples.
- Bring to a boil, cover, then cook for 10 – 15 minutes on high heat, until the apples are tender.
- Turn off the heat and blend the content. Set aside.
- Add 6l of water and sugar to a separate pot, and bring to a boil while stirring frequently.
- When the water boils, add in the blended apples and bring the combined content to a boil again. Cook for 5 min then turn off the heat.
- Strain the juice through a strainer or a strainer or thin cotton cloth or filter. Discard the solid parts and serve some juice immediately.

Save the remaining content in well-closed glass bottles or jars, for several months.

Blended Beet and Potato Soup

| Prep time: 5 min | Cook time: 40 min | Servings: 1 |

Ingredients

- *Peeled, cooked, and cubed beets (4 medium sizes)*
- *Peeled and cubed potatoes (4 medium sizes)*
- *Dried dill (1 tsp)*
- *Dairy-free milk or fat-free evaporated milk (½ cup)*
- *Vegetable stock (8 cups)*
- *Salt*
- *Pepper*

Instructions

- Add beets and cubed potatoes to the non-stick pan and stir for a couple of minutes to catch some color.

- Add in the stock.
- Bring to a boil, then reduce the heat and simmer.
- Cook the content for 30 – 40 minutes until very softened.
- Blend the content to achieve consistency.
- Add milk and stir.
- Add salt and pepper to taste.

Potato Spinach Soup

| Prep time: 10 min | Cook time: 50 min | Servings: 1 |

Ingredients

- *Flour (¼ cup)*
- *Large onion (½ bulb)*
- *Ghee butter (1 tbsp)*
- *Salt (2 tsp)*
- *Peeled and cubed potatoes (2 cups)*
- *Evaporated skim milk (½ cup)*

- *Chopped spinach (frozen or fresh) (1 cup)*
- *Water (3 cups)*

Instructions

- Melt butter in a non-stick pan.
- Add onions and cook for 10 minutes until tender, stirring occasionally.
- Add water, potatoes, and salt.
- Stir the content as it boils.
- Lower the temperature and allow the content to simmer for 30 minutes.
- Add spinach and cook for approx. 5 minutes until cooked.
- Puree the content using a blender or food processor.
- Stir in the milk to the content.

Tips: You could decide to go all liquid with your lunch rather than dwelling on solids.

Carrot Soup

| Prep time: 20 min | Cook time: 1 h | Servings: 6 |

Ingredients

- *1 tbsp avocado oil*
- *1 onion, peeled and chopped*
- *salt and freshly ground black pepper*
- *1-pound carrots, peeled and sliced*
- *1 large sweet potato, peeled and diced*
- *2 bay leaves*
- *6 cups of chicken stock / vegetable stock or water*

Instructions

- Heat the oil in a large saucepan over medium heat.
- Add the onion and stir occasionally, until tender but not golden, 8 to 10 minutes. Season with salt and pepper.

- Add the carrot, sweet potato, bay leaves and 5 cups of vegetable broth. Cover the pot. Cook 30 to 45 minutes, until the vegetables are very tender.
- Remove the bay leaves. Blend the soup in a blender or food processor until very smooth. Add some of the remaining broth if the soup is too thick.
- Season with salt and pepper. Serve hot.

Tips: Freeze your soup and make it a quick last-minute meal. Simply double whatever recipe you are following. Just cook all parts of the soup that need it, let it cool to room temperature, and then put it in freezer!

Potato and Turnip

| Prep time: 10 min | Cook time: 20 min | Servings: 2 |

Ingredients

- *Large red new potatoes (6)*
- *Large turnips (2)*
- *Warm chicken broth (½ cup)*
- *Plain Greek yogurt (0% fat) or non-fat sour cream (½ cup)*
- *Salt and pepper*

Instructions

- Peel the potatoes and turnips.
- Slice them to achieve a thickness of ¼ inch.
- Boil the content for 15 – 20 minutes until tender.
- Drain the content and whip to achieve consistency.
- Include yogurt/sour cream and warm chicken broth in the content.
- Season the mixture with pepper and salt. Whip the mixture again to achieve consistency.

4-WEEKS MEAL PLAN

1st Week Meal Plan

Day	Breakfast	Snack	Lunch	Dinner	Dessert
1	Banana Walnut Pancakes	Berry-Mint Smoothie	Ginger Glazed Tuna	Garlicky Barley and Pinto Beans	Almond Apple Smoothie
2	Banana Quinoa	Celery Juice	Grilled turkey Teriyaki	Kale and cottage Pasta	Immunity Boosting Smoothie
3	Zucchini Chips with Parmesan Cheese	Cucumber Breeze Smoothie	Elegant Turkey Roast	Glazed Tempeh	Raspberry Cobbler
4	Crab, Dill Fritters	Watermelon Smoothie	Chicken Chili	Mahi-Mahi Salad-Stuffed Avocado	Green Monster
5	Almond Apple Smoothie	Banana Quinoa	Cod Salad with Eggs	Vegetable Stew	Baked Pears with Quinoa
6	Mixed Flour Banana Bread	Immunity-Boosting Smoothie	Couscous Salad	Ginger Tempeh and Vegetable Stir-Fry	Warm Apple Juice
7	Breakfast Farro Porridge	Cod Salad with Eggs	Glazed Tempeh	Grilled Turkey Teriyaki	Green Tea Maple Syrup Frozen Yogurt

2nd Week Meal Plan

Day	Breakfast	Snack	Lunch	Dinner	Dessert
1	Green Monster	Couscous Salad	Baked Chicken with Barley	Turkey and Orzo Soup	Coconut Mug Brownie
2	Beet and Strawberry Smoothie	Banana Quinoa	Kale and cottage Pasta	Garlicky Barley and Pinto Beans	Blueberry Oats Bars
3	Cod Salad with Eggs	Celery Juice	Maple syrup-Orange Glazed Salmon	Meatballs with Ginger	Orange Sesame Seed Biscotti
4	Millet Barley Pancakes	Citrus Tangy - Boosting Smoothie	Lamb with Pears in Crockpot	Fresh Kale Garlic Soup	Butternut Squash Pie
5	Citrus Tangy Boosting Smoothie	Mixed Flour Banana Bread	Couscous Salad	Carrot and Zucchini Soup	Papaya and Mint Sorbet
6	Carrot Juice, 1 apple, crackers	Cranberry-Ginger Smoothie	Vegetable Stew	Garlic Turkey Breasts with Lemon	Warm Apple Juice
7	Pomegranate blackberry Smoothie	Crab, Dill Fritters	Ginger Glazed Tuna	Baked Chicken with Barley	Almon Apple Smoothie

3rd Week Meal Plan

Day	Breakfast	Snack	Lunch	Dinner	Dessert
1	Maple syrup-glazed herbed sweet potatoes	Cranberry-Ginger Smoothie	Cod Salad with Eggs	Ginger Tempeh and Vegetable Stir-Fry	Yummy Red dragon fruit Sorbet
2	Celery Juice, crackers, 1 banana	Stuffed Mushrooms with Herbs	Baked Chicken with Barley	Mahi-Mahi Salad-Stuffed Avocado	Pecans-Cinnamon Pumpkin Custards
3	Breakfast Farro Porridge	Cod Salad with Eggs	Lamb with Pears in Crockpot	Carrot and Zucchini Soup	Chilled Banana Pudding
4	Almond Apple Smoothie	Crab, Dill Fritters	Baked Chicken with Barley	Red Lentil and chickpeas Soup	Nutmeg Apple Frozen Yogurt
5	Pumpkin-Pears Smoothie	Couscous Salad	Garlic Turkey Breasts with Lemon	Maple syrup-Orange Glazed Salmon	Cucumber Breeze Smoothie
6	Spinach Protein Smoothie	Chicken Tenders with Pineapple	Egg Fried Quinoa	Baked Chicken with Barley	Green Monster
7	Strawberry-Raspberry Smoothie	Carrot Juice	Couscous Salad	Grilled Turkey Teriyaki	Fruit Kebabs

4th Week Meal Plan

Day	Breakfast	Snack	Lunch	Dinner	Dessert
1	Apple muffins with cinnamon	Fresh Fruit Kebabs	Ginger Tempeh and Vegetable Stir-Fry	Grilled turkey Teriyaki	Blueberry Oats Bars
2	Breakfast Farro Porridge	Mermaid Smoothie Bowl	Creamy Broccoli and Sweet Potato Soup	Maple Syrup-Orange Glazed Salmon	Warm Apple Juice with pulp
3	Millet Barley Pancakes	Pumpkin-Pears Smoothie	Mahi-Mahi Salad-Stuffed Avocado	Meatballs with Ginger	Green Tea Peaches Smoothie
4	Banana Cauliflower Smoothie	Crab, Dill Fritters	Garlic Turkey Breasts with Lemon	Red Lentil and Chickpeas Soup	Mini Fruit Pizzas in Pears
5	Carrot Juice, 1 Banana	Buckwheat Strawberry Pancake	Lamb with Pears in Crockpot	Glazed Tempeh	Chocolate Cookies without Flour
6	Chicken Tenders with Pineapple	Couscous Salad	Hemp Broiled Tilapia with Ginger	Turkey and Orzo Soup	Ginger Oat Breads
7	Green Tea-Peaches Smoothie	Crab, Dill Fritters	Vegetable Stew	Chicken Chili	Green Monster